SSPU New Syllabus

A Book of

INTRODUCTION TO SOCIAL PSYCHOLOGY

for

F.Y. B.A. Psychology (Semester - II)
New Syllabus as per CBCS Pattern,
June 2019

Dr. Anuradha Prashant Harkare
M.A. (Psychology), M.Sc., Ph.D. (Chemistry), B.Ed.
Assistant Professor
Dr. D.Y. Patil College of Arts, Commerce & Science
Pimpri, Pune 411018

NIRALI PRAKASHAN
ADVANCEMENT OF KNOWLEDGE

N5149

Inroduction to Social Psychology **ISBN 978-93-89686-21-0**
First Edition : November 2019

Published By:
NIRALI PRAKASHAN
Abhyudaya Pragati, 1312, Shivaji Nagar
Off J.M. Road, PUNE – 411005
Tel - (020) 25512336/37/39, Fax - (020) 25511379
Email : niralipune@pragationline.com

➢ DISTRIBUTION CENTRES

PUNE

Nirali Prakashan (For orders within Pune) : 119, Budhwar Peth, Jogeshwari Mandir Lane, Pune 411002, Maharashtra, Tel : (020) 2445 2044, Mobile : 9657703145
Email : niralilocal@pragationline.com

Nirali Prakashan (For orders outside Pune) : S. No. 28/27, Dhayari, Near Asian College Pune 411041
Tel : (020) 24690204; Mobile : 9657703143
Email : bookorder@pragationline.com

MUMBAI

Nirali Prakashan : 385, S.V.P. Road, Rasdhara Co-op. Hsg. Society Ltd., Girgaum, Mumbai 400004, Maharashtra;
Mobile : 9320129587 Tel : (022) 2385 6339 / 2386 9976,
Fax : (022) 2386 9976
Email : niralimumbai@pragationline.com

➢ DISTRIBUTION BRANCHES

JALGAON

Nirali Prakashan : 34, V. V. Golani Market, Navi Peth, Jalgaon 425001, Maharashtra, Tel : (0257) 222 0395, Mob : 94234 91860;
Email : niralijalgaon@pragationline.com

KOLHAPUR

Nirali Prakashan : New Mahadvar Road, Kedar Plaza, 1st Floor Opp. IDBI Bank, Kolhapur 416 012, Maharashtra. Mob : 9850046155;
Email : niralikolhapur@pragationline.com

NAGPUR

Nirali Prakashan : Above Maratha Mandir, Shop No. 3, First Floor, Rani Jhanshi Square, Sitabuldi, Nagpur 440012, Maharashtra
Tel : (0712) 254 7129;
Email : niralinagpur@pragationline.com

DELHI

Nirali Prakashan : 4593/15, Basement, Agarwal Lane, Ansari Road, Daryaganj Near Times of India Building, New Delhi 110002
Mob : 08505972553, Email : niralidelhi@pragationline.com

BENGALURU

Nirali Prakashan : Maitri Ground Floor, Jaya Apartments, No. 99, 6th Cross, 6th Main, Malleswaram, Bengaluru 560003, Karnataka;
Mob : 9449043034
Email: niralibangalore@pragationline.com

Other Branches : Hyderabad, Chennai

niralipune@pragationline.com | www.pragationline.com

Also find us on f www.facebook.com/niralibooks

Preface ...

The Ministry of Human Resource Development (HRD), Govt. of India, have initiated the process for developing New Education Policy (NEP) in our country to bring out reforms in Indian education system. The process of syllabus revision will be helpful in developing students' personalities. The UGC has already initiated several steps to bring equity, efficiency and academic excellence in National Higher Education System.

Changing and updating the syllabus for first-year Arts (Psychology) starting with academic year2019-20 is one of the steps to cope with the upcoming changes and advancements in Psychology.

With beginning of this academic year along with the syllabus, one more change is introduced. The academic year will have two semesters. The marks per semester (100) will be divided into a 70-30 pattern. There will be 70 marks for semester end exam and 30 marks will be for internal evaluation. Further, these 30 marks will be divided into, 20 marks for mid-semester examination and 10 marks for home assignment, orals, lecture notes, or a project work.

This choice-based credit system will lead to a comprehensive assessment of the students.

This year, inclusion of Social Psychology is one of the important changes.

This textbook is designed in accordance with the new syllabus and more emphasis is placed in using simple language. The goal of writing this textbook is to focus on students and motivate them to learn and understand the basics and further build upon the introduction to social psychology. The real-life examples given in the book will make the various concepts easy to relate and understand.

I am sure, as Social Psychology being a fascinating subject, not only the students but also the psychology lovers will also find this book interesting to read and assimilate the learning.

I am grateful to Dr. Snehal Agnihotri, Principal; Dr. Ranjit Patil, Vice Principal; and Dr. Gauri Kadam, Head of the Psychology department- Dr. D Y Patil Arts, Commerce and Science College, Pimpri, Pune for their support and encouragement.

I would be failing if I don't acknowledge the support of my family members. I am deeply thankful to them as without their help this book might not have been possible.

I express my sincere thanks to **Mr. Dineshbhai Furia** and **Mr. Jignesh Furia** of Nirali Prakashan, Pune for having published this book. A special thanks to **Mrs. Varsha Bodake** and **Mrs. Sharda Bhandarge** for their valueable contribution to this book.

Any suggestions from students and teachers for further improvement of this book shall be welcome.

PUNE **AUTHOR**

November 2019

☆☆☆

Syllabus ...

1. **INTRODUCTION**
   - 1.1 Definition, Brief History of Social Psychology (Indian Context)
   - 1.2 Scope of Social Psychology
   - 1.3 Levels of Social Behavior
   - 1.4 Approaches Towards Understanding Social Behaviour
   - 1.5 Application : Community Mental Health
2. **INDIVIDUAL LEVEL PROCESSES**
   - 2.1 Difference Between Social Cognition and Social Perception
   - 2.2 Self-Concept : Nature, Self-regulation and Self-presentation
   - 2.3 Attitude : Definition, Components, Dimensions and Formation of Attitude
   - 2.4 Prejudice : Causes
   - 2.5 Application : Formation of Attitude and Prejudice Eradication
3. **INTERPERSONAL PROCESSES**
   - 3.1 Interpersonal Attraction, Love
   - 3.2 Pro-social Behaviour
   - 3.3 Locus of Control, Increasing Our Helping Nature
   - 3.4 Aggression : Meaning, Nature and Causes of Aggression
   - 3.5 Application : Prevention and Reducing Aggression
4. **GROUP DYNAMICS**
   - 4.1 Groups : When we Join and when we Leave, The Benefits of Joining
   - 4.2 Co-operation and Conflict
   - 4.3 Conformity, Factors Affecting Conformity, Obedience and Authority
   - 4.4 Group Decision Making
   - 4.5 Application : Team Building

☆☆☆

Contents ...

1. Introduction to Social Psychology ***1.1 – 1.16***

1.1 Introduction
1.2 Scope of Social Psychology
1.3 Levels of Social Behavior
1.4 Approaches towards Understanding Social Bahavior
1.5 Application: Community Mental Health

2. Individual Level Processes ***2.1 – 2.28***

2.1 Difference between Social Cognition and Social Perception
2.2 "Self" - Concept
2.3 Attitude (Evaluating Social World)
2.4 Prejudice
2.5 Applications: Attitude Formation and Prejudice Eradication

3. Interpersonal Processes ***3.1 – 3.34***

3.1 Introduction
3.2 Pro-Social Bahavior - Helping Others
3.3 Locus of Control
3.4 Aggression
3.5 Application: Prevention and Reducing Aggression

4. Group Dynamics ***4.1 – 4.34***

4.1 Groups
4.2 Cooperation and Conflict
4.3 Social Influence
4.4 Group Decision Making
4.5 Application : Team Building

Model Question Paper

Reference Books

☆☆☆

UNIT – 1

INTRODUCTION TO SOCIAL PSYCHOLOGY

SYNOPSIS

1.1 Introduction

1.1.1 Nature and Definition

1.1.2 A brief History of Social Psychology

1.2 Scope of Social Psychology

1.3 Levels of Social Behavior

1.3.1 Individual Behavior

1.3.2 Interpersonal Behavior

1.3.3 Group Behavior

1.4 Approaches towards Understanding Social Bahavior

1.4.1 Psychodynamic Approach

1.4.2 Behavioral Approach

1.4.3 Cognitive Approach

1.4.4 Socio-Cultural Approach

1.5 Application: Community Mental Health

1.5.1 Community Mental Health Promotion and Protection

✧ Exercise

1.1 Introduction

Remember the incidence you have witnessed on road, where in an accident two people are fighting instead of finding emergency help and few others who have no concern are watching unnecessarily. After any speech or performance; if one of the audiences stand up to offer standing ovation, others also support that behavior and stand, irrespective of whether they like it or not. An old lady is waiting to cross a busy road, but out of a large number of people present around, hardly one or two offer help. When there is stone-pelting, a person who is not very aggressive or hostile otherwise also gets engaged in that activity.

Fig. 1.1: People fighting on the road

Do you wonder why do people behave the way they behave? Have you ever questioned why do you portray yourself differently in front of people than when you are alone? You will get the answers to such questions in this stream of psychology called social psychology.

As Aristotle- the well known Greek philosopher said, "Man is by nature a social animal; an individual who is unsocial naturally and not accidentally is either beneath our notice or more than human. Society is something that precedes the individual." This quote reveals the importance of society.

The study of human psychology hence is the study of social psychology. It is about understanding individual behavior in a social context.

For this reason, it can be said that social psychology came into existence when human beings started living together. Thus social psychology may be considered as old as Homo sapiens on this planet.

Though people used to live together with family, community, they may not have learned to live together in harmony in serenity. No wonder ancient thinkers and philosophers like Aristotle and Plato as well as Gautam Buddha, Chanakya and many more were in search of peace.

This chapter reveals the nature, scope of social psychology and approaches to study the same. It also throws light on applications of social psychology in community mental health.

1.1.1 Nature and Definition

As human beings are social; we live with others. In every interaction, either we influence the other or get influenced by others. Thus social psychologists study those factors that force to behave in a particular manner in the presence of others, factors which persuade us to change our thinking and behavior. Manuscripts on social psychology in the modern period came into existence when in 1908 William McDougall published a book in English titled 'An introduction to Social Psychology'. As per his views, social behavior was innate and hence individualistic. However, this belief was not accepted by many. Social psychology has been defined by various psychologists and philosophers as follows.

- It is the scientific attempt to understand and explain how the thought, feeling, and behavior of individuals are influenced by the actual, imagined, or implied the presence of others. - **Allport (1954).**
- It is a study of inter social stimulation and response, social attitudes, values, and personalities. **- Bogardus (1924).**
- It is the study of an individual's behavior in groups and how an individual's behavior, feelings, and thoughts are influenced by others. **- Kimble Young.**
- It is the discipline that studies human behavior and mental processes. **- R.S. Feldman.**
- **Kurt Lewin**, known as a father of modern social psychology gave the definition as: It is the scientific study of an individual's behavior in social situations.

1.1.2 A Brief History of Social Psychology

Aristotle considered that it is the basis of our inborn nature that we adhere to positive affiliations and collective ways of living. After viewing the development of social psychology one cannot ignore the influence of thinkers like John Locke, David Hume, Comte and so forth in 17th, 18th and 19th century.

But social psychology gained recognition as a distinct form of psychology after Darwin's theory of evolution has been propagated. In 1860 a journal, "Folk Psychology" was started by Lazarus; while in 1901, E. Ross published his most famous works, social control, in which he analyzed societal stability in terms of sympathy, sociability and social justice. In 1945, Kurt Lewin founded 'The American Sociometric Society'. Since then social psychology was one of the subjects of attraction for many. Hence he is considered as the father of modern social psychology. Leon Festinger, Solomon Asch, Fritz Heider, Stanley Milgram, and Sherif Muzafer are few of the very famous experimental psychologists who laid a great impact on social psychology.

History from Indian Context:

Ancient India: Roots of social psychology in the Indian culture can be seen as early as 1500 B.C.

The manuscripts such as the *Vedas*, the *Upanishads*, the *Puranas*, and epics like the *Mahabharata,* the *Ramayana* contain social, economic, and political insights that are applicable even for the present social reality.

In your childhood, you must have read stories from *'Panchtantra, Hitopdesh,* and *Jatak Katha*. They were none other than the learning of social behavior. *Panchtantra* which is a collection of animal fables was written by Pandit Vishnu Sharma who taught all the necessary social skills, political and practical wisdom to three sons of a King called Amarshakti.

Fig. 1.2: *Panchtantra* and Teaching of Social behavior

The *Jatak* tales are a collection of Buddhist stories of wisdom. Islamic culture too provides an idea of brotherhood concerning social life. The Sufi saints emphasize the valuable doctrine of *sabr* (patience) while understanding others. Very popular *Dohas* by great poet Kabir give insight about the equality of human beings.

Modern India: During the pre-independence period, Indian culture was influenced by a series of religious, political, and social reform movements headed by Swami Vivekanand, Lokmanya Tilak, Mahatma Gandhi, Raja Ram Mohan Roy and many more. Their thoughts were a great source of societal restructuring.

From a psychological and applied point of view beginning of social psychology can be traced out in the 1920s when in Calcutta, psychology was considered as a scientific discipline and the department of psychology came into existence. Culcutta University established the first department of psychology in 1916. Dr. Narendra Nath Sengupta was the first chairman of the department. Though he was an experimental psychologist, he showed a keen interest in Indian society. Later he worked with one of the most eminent sociologists Radhakamal Mukherjee from Lucknow University. In 1928 he produced a book on social psychology.

After him, the renowned psychoanalyst of that time Dr. Girindrasekhar Bose headed the department who also established the 'Indian Psychoanalytical Society'. After Calcutta, psychology departments were established later in Mysore in 1924 and Patna in 1946.

Since then gradual development in various streams of psychology was observed but it was under the influence of western schools of thought. However, Dr. Girindrsekhar Bose took efforts to link the western approaches with Indian culture.

Social psychology in pre-independence time was a little less popular than in general psychology and clinical psychology. But post-independence, it grew in popularity. Prejudice, stereotypes and social attitudes were popularly studied. Other areas like intergroup relations, deprivation, and leadership were also of interest. Irrespective of progress in social psychological research in India, it didn't show a distinct change because understanding of Indian reality was carried through western concepts. Along with, enough amount of data showed that social psychological theories developed in the west, did not offer a solution to complex problems of social change and progress in India.

Later Prof. Durganand Sinha showed that though Indian psychology, which was almost completely western in its orientation, is gradually changing its approach and adapting to the socio-cultural context of India. Prof. Sinha was a visionary who gave Indian psychology a new direction and identity via his influential writings and efforts in the areas of indigenous psychology. Social psychology today is broadening its field by the research work on touching various aspects of life such as population psychology, health psychology, environmental psychology, criminal and legal psychology, etc. Now it also has taken up a multicultural outlook to understand behavior concerning cultural and social context.

Social psychology today has become much more relevant to the understanding of interpersonal relations and everyday life. It is throwing more light as well on human thinking and attitudes which will lead to a better socially managed life. Multicultural perspective, cognitive approach, sociobiology, and evolutionary psychology are some of the current movements in social psychology.

1.2 Scope of Social Psychology

Social psychology is a scientific and systematic study of human behavior in society. As it attempts to understand the socio-psychological causes and motives of an individual's behavior in the group, hence the individual and society can be considered as a complete system. Also, we can analyze the interrelations, their interdependence and developmental functions of both- the individual and the society. In the modern world, this branch of psychology finds great importance in all walks of life. The scope of social psychology can be seen in the following areas.

1. **Social Psychology and Health:** In the modern world many of the mental disorders are growing fast. Problems like stress, depression, anxiety, psychosis are on the rise. Most of the mental health problems have socio-psychological causes such as cutthroat competitions, increased demands and expectations from every relation, burden of performance, fragile relations, stressful working conditions and like. Unfortunately, the coping ways are getting faulty and hence people are getting engaged in drug abuse, emotional disturbance, self-harm, etc. Social psychologists try to explore the basis of these problems and work independently or in collaboration with social workers, psychiatrists for the well being of an individual.

2. **Social Psychology and Education:** To improve teaching techniques, learning practices, cognitive skills, the motivation of students, and also teacher-student relationship; social psychologist plays a critical role. Many times poor academic performance can be due to socio-psychological issues like lack of motivation, punishments, fear of failure in the exam, parental pressure, low socioeconomic status, unavailability of resources, etc. It also guides how to cope with test anxiety. Social psychology helps to find the gaps and bridge them.

3. **Social Psychology and Industry:** The industrial sector is one of the most effective sectors in building the economy of the nation. Better working conditions, good employer-employee relation has a direct effect on productivity. Social psychology helps to deal with issues like absenteeism, strike, motivation, etc. Effective use of token economy, bonus, etc. are also studied in social psychology.

Along with these above mentioned areas, social psychology finds its influential role to play in other areas like women psychology, military psychology, criminal psychology, multicultural issues. The scope of social psychology also may be studied from various aspects such as consequences of the situation, the influence of a person, the cognitive abilities of an individual, etc.

1.3 Levels of Social Bahavior

Social psychology being subject to the study of human behavior in the social context studies the reason behind any behavior. What causes or motivates us to behave in a certain way? Why few people are great leaders? How we develop various opinions and prejudices about events, situations, and people. All such questions can be answered if one studies the interaction between two or more people. Social behavior consists of a set of interactions among individuals. Social psychology tries to analyze the social behavior on three levels. They are as follows-

1.3.1 Individual Behavior

Any behavior is considered as a result of the transaction. Behavior comes in many forms such as eating, sleeping, reading, following traffic rules, etc. Individual behavior means some concrete action by a person. Certain individual characteristics are responsible for the way a person behaves in daily life situations as well as reacts to any emergencies. His behavior is influenced by various factors such as his needs, motivation, personality traits, past experiences, socioeconomic status, and ability and like. The individualistic behavior is controlled by other extrinsic aspects as environmental and organizational factors. Factors such as gender, race, culture, attitude, incidents, etc are too responsible to cause the behavior. An individual who is a total gentleman may get vengeful when someone harms him badly. Or when a person greets another, in response another person also greets.

Famous social psychologist Kurt Lewin stated the field theory and outlined the behavior framework. The theory is expressed using the formula which states that behavior is a function of the person and his/her environment.

$$B = f(P, E)$$

where, B - Behavior, P - Person, E - Environment, f - function of

For example, a married person behaves differently when gets divorced. In the field theory, he stated that a persons' life space determines their behavior.

Social psychologists may help to improve the behavior of an individual in need. School counselors facilitate students to handle stress and enhance their quality of life.

1.3.2 Interpersonal Behavior

The individual learns how to behave by observation. Our behavior is influenced by people surrounding us. If you find someone smiling at you, in response you also give a smile.

Fig. 1.3: Two friends waving at each other

If you find traffic police standing at a signal, you try to follow the traffic rules. His presence makes you behave in a certain manner. We follow the dressing fashion, talking style of a person whom we are impressed by. The decision of taking a course like psychology for graduation might be influenced by your friend's decision to take the same. Many students take courses like engineering for further studies because of parental pressure. After listening to any motivational speech, thinking of people changes. During the freedom fight, a huge number of people used to get influenced by reading inspirational articles.

You must have experienced watching a cricket match alone or sometimes with family or friends. Did you find the difference in enjoyment? You enjoy more with others.

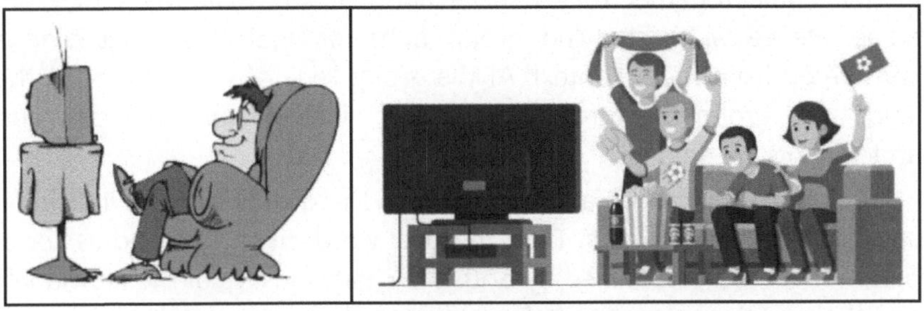

Fig. 1.4: Enjoying any sports alone and with family

The presence of others makes a huge impact on our life. We will remain meaningless without people and society.

Emotions like anger, jealousy, joy, pride, love, and many more are only because of reference of someone other. Competition, cooperation, compliance, etc. are possible since there is another person involved.

Communication can be considered as interpersonal behavior as well.

Every individual encounters many others as per the situation and need. A working person encounters his boss, colleagues, subordinates, and clients. A student interacts with teachers, friends and examiner. A person who is ill gets in touch with nurses, doctors, other patients, etc.

Out of many people around, we relate more closely with only a few. Sometimes we get a chance to interact with people for a very less time, still we may like or may not like them. To have a friendship with or to fall in love with some specific person what factors must be responsible? What are the reasons which keep us bonded with our beloved ones?

Every individual after working for long hours or traveling for long-distance wants to go home and meet his beloved ones. Everyone craves for love and care. An individual's quality of life matters a lot because of presence of others. You also must have experienced that if you come to college after having some arguments with your parents, you stay unhappy and unable to concentrate. If a person is not happy or satisfied with family relations, then his performance also gets affected.

When people get well along with each other, productivity in general increases. The interpersonal aspect of human behavior is extremely important for having harmony in society.

1.3.3 Group Behavior

The psychology of the group is very complex. When more than two people come together they behave another way than when they are alone. Hence while studying group behavior; individuals' behavior is considered from social context. At the group level of social behavior, the study of group gestures, intra-group, inter-group conflicts, and attachments are studied.

The behavior can be affected by both the qualities of the individual and the situational factors. Thus, in other words, it can be said as social behavior can be determined by both the characteristics of the individuals and the situations they are in. For example, during a natural calamity like floods, many people from upper socioeconomic status have to stay in refugee camps and wait for food.

Fig. 1.5: Rescue team helping during flood

As social psychology helps to understand people's behavior, it takes efforts to study change in behavior of a person in group. For example, a person who may not be interested in fasting as a ritual, but he has to follow social norms and hence keeps fasting even if hungry.

An army officer fights for his country even though he is on the verge of death. Why an individual behaves the way he or she behaves in social context? Social behavior has various aspects and is characterized by complexity. Human behavior is highly influenced by social norms.

There is no restriction on the member size of a group, but as the size increases, its influence also increases. When a single member of the group goes against the norms, he or she has to face extreme consequences. The example of honor killing can be put as an intense example of social pressure. Even while going to a dinner at a party or a specific worship place, one has to follow the dress code. Asking for dowry, not allowing for inter-cast marriage, forced to wear a specific style of clothes, and many more are examples of social behavior.

Ideally, group behavior must be following security and peace of society, but increasing involvement of religious aspect is making the social psychologist to worry. The group mentality is difficult to understand. It cannot be controlled by oppression and domination. To control the agitated group is a very difficult and challenging task for the people who deal with it. The mass mentality is very unpredictable. To understand it remains one of the major goals of social psychology.

Social psychology analyses human behavior also from the following three levels. These are – (1) Biological level of analysis, (2) Cognitive level of analysis, and (3) Socio-cultural level of analysis.

1. The Biological Level: It talks about the physiological explanation of human behavior. It focuses on the influence of the brain, nervous system, neurotransmitters, hormones, genetics, etc. For example, an increase in testosterone hormone in response to anger have been reported in many research's inferences.

2. Cognitive Level: This level explains the behavior from the mental processes point of view. The way an individual from this perspective sees the world and the experiences he had in his life have an impact on his or her behavior. For example, if a woman gets repeatedly abused by her husband, then she may get angry with males in general. If a person takes an effort to achieve, then he believes that hard work is a key to success.

3. Socio-Cultural Level: According to this level, human behavior is because of the influence of society. Race, ethnicity, gender, religion, and cultural norms decide the guidelines for human's most of the behavior. For example, in our society, a girl is expected to do household chores. Or some cultures allow males and females to mingle freely in public places; others do not. Similarly, in some cultures remarriages after demise of the partner is not encouraged, but in some cultures remarriages are considered as a usual practice.

1.4 Approaches towards Understanding Social Behavior

Human or social behavior is explained with the help of various approaches. Some of them are discussed as follows.

1.4.1 Psychodynamic Approach

Sigmund Freud put this approach to explain human behavior which had a tremendous impact on the field of psychology. He argued that the mind has three levels of consciousness. Out of those, the unconscious mind is the primary source of human behavior. The inaccessible unconscious mind influences judgments, feelings, or behavior. He also stated that human behavior is motivated from the interplay of 'id' which works on the pleasure principle, 'ego' which works on reality principal and 'superego' which works on moral principle. According to him one cannot ignore the role of potent internal instincts and drives. Psychodynamic approach states that childhood experiences have an immense impact on individuals' personality to shape. Personality and behavior are the results of interactions of three parts of mind i.e. the id, ego, and superego.

Fig. 1.6: Exploring unconscious to understand personality

According to Freud, defense mechanisms used by people to cope with anxiety, or slip of tongue are also because of unconscious thoughts. For example, when a person who got scolded by his boss in the office, shouts at the children or wife at home, then he is using displacement mechanism as a defense.

1.4.2 Behavioral Approach

This approach was initiated and popularized by Ivan Pavlov, B.F. Skinner, Watson, and others. This approach contradicts the role of the unconscious, feelings, or desires. It studies observable behavior without understanding the internal processes that create it. This approach tells that using a set of instructions and putting various conditions, change can be generated in human or animal behavior. According to behaviorism, any learning is possible and any behavior can be modified. This approach also addresses various types of motivations that direct specific behavior. Behavior change interventions need to consider specific psychological and social influences that guide decision making and behavior in a particular setting. For example, a frustrated person will tend to behave aggressively.

1.4.3 Cognitive Approach

The cognitive approach is a relatively modern approach to human behavior that focuses on how we think. It studies human thinking and its relationships with social behavior and assumes that our thought process affects how we think. It studies those processes which influence people's social perception, judgment, and behavior. These processes can be involved in social interactions at a group level or on the individual level. Ulric Neisser proposed in his book 'Cognitive Psychology' that the human mind works similarly to computers.

The cognitive approach attempts to apply a scientific way to understand human behavior.

1.4.4 Socio-Cultural Approach

This approach explores how a specific culture influences the way we think and learn. It focuses on the interdependence of human behavior and societal, cultural influence. Nationality, gender, religion, socio-economic status, cultural traditions, age, and peer group, etc have an impact on an individual's behavior. Do individuals from low economic strata get more in crime? Do families, who eat together, stay together? Does unemployment is a reason for depression? Why do many people follow the path of any charismatic person? The socio-cultural approach tries to find answers to such questions. Socio-cultural perspective can also help to understand different interpretations from various cultural points of view. For example, to ask a question to a single mother whether she is married or not can be offensive in one culture but it can be a routine issue in another.

1.5 Application: Community Mental Health

According to the definition given by WHO (World Health Organization), "Health is a state of complete physical, mental, and social well-being and not merely the absence of disease or infirmity." The most important suggestion of this definition is that mental health is more than just an absence of mental disorder or disability. Mental health is a state of well being in which an individual understands his or her abilities, can cope with normal stresses of life, can work more productively and can contribute to the community.

It can be considered as persons' and hence alternatively communities' combined ability to think, interact, and enjoy life. Thus every individual contributes in maintaining the community's mental health.

Social, psychological, physical and spiritual well being of a person determines the level of mental health of the community. Individuals with these problems are vulnerable to mental health problems. For example, constant socio-economic stress and violence are known as risk factors. Poor mental health has a strong correlation with gender discrimination, sexual exploitation, damaging lifestyle, stressful work conditions, consistent financial constraints, physical illness, etc.

A social psychologist may help in finding various such causes responsible for the poor mental health of the community and try to put forward possible remedy on the same. People should be given training for coping with adverse conditions and uplifting their quality of life.

1.5.1 Community Mental Health Promotion and Protection

People are the integral part of society. Hence for the smooth and harmonious running of it, well being of people is of the highest importance.

Promotion and protection of the mental health of the community can be achieved in various ways. Priority must be given to make people aware and educate them accordingly.

This can be achieved in three parts.

Firstly, awareness and education of the people, secondly encouraging the people to take help and treatment for existing mental ill health, and thirdly training the people to cope with adverse conditions and situations to avoid mental ill-health.

Some of the ways to protect and promote mental health include –

- Safe and stable environment to children with protection from threats and abuse. Provide equal opportunities for schooling.
- Social - economical empowerment of women.
- Social support for the elderly population, people from minorities, migrants, victims of disasters, etc.
- Promotion of human rights and community development programs.
- Training of parents and teachers to address behavioral changes in children and students.
- Working on changing the attitude of people to hide mental problems.

Fig. 1.7: Need of Availability of mental health centers

Along with these, effective measures also must be taken in the treatment of mental disorders. Easy availability of mental health doctors and trainers in the remote areas is one of the biggest issues. Also, the taboo behind mental ill health pushes people to take the help of an exorcist. Educating these people is an essential task.

Briefly, it can be said that the overall action plan for promoting mental health must be to prevent mental disorder, provide care, enhance recovery, and promote human rights.

To achieve these goals, there must be collaboration among government, NGOs, social workers, mental health practitioners, and every citizen. If every stakeholder of society works accordingly, no doubt there will be harmony in the community.

✧ Exercise ✧

Q. 1 : Answer the following questions in 100 words :

(1) *What is meant by social psychology?*

(2) *Explain the nature of social psychology.*

(3) *How social psychology is studied using biological level of analysis?*

Q. 2 : Answer the following questions in 200 words :

(1) *How modern psychology was under the influence of Western Psychology?*

(2) *Explain how the medical and educations sectors work in social psychology.*

(3) *Which are the ways to study individual behavior?*

Q. 3 : Answer the following questions in 400 words :

(1) *Elaborate how the behavior of an individual changes his behavior as per Kurt Lewin's equation.*

(2) *Which is the behavoristic view of studying social psychology?*

(3) *How the individual's behavior is influenced by social pressure?*

(4) *How the interpersonal behavior get influenced because of society?*

Q. 4 : Write short notes :

(1) *Standing of social psychology in ancient Indian psychology.*

(2) *Psychoanalytic theory and social behavior of human beings.*

(3) *Community mental health.*

✧ Questions from Previous University Exams ✧

(1) *What is social psychology? Explain theories in social psychology.* **(Oct. 2011)**

(2) *Write a note on application of social psychology and health.* **(Oct. 2011)**

(3) *What are the three levels of behavior?* **(April 2015)**

(4) *Describe the related fields of social psychology.* **(April 2015)**

☆☆☆

UNIT – 2

Individual Level Processes

SYNOPSIS

2.1 *Difference between Social Cognition and Social Perception*

2.1.1 Social Cognition

2.1.2 Social Perception

2.2 *"Self" - Concept*

2.2.1 Definitions of Self-Concept

2.2.2 Nature

2.2.3 Self-Regulation

2.2.4 Self-Presentation

2.3 *Attitude (Evaluating Social World)*

2.3.1 Definitions of Attitude

2.3.2 Components of Attitude

2.3.3 Dimensions of Attitude

2.3.4 Formation of Attitude

2.4 *Prejudice*

2.4.1 Causes

2.5 *Applications: Attitude Formation and Prejudice Eradication*

2.5.1 Attitude Formation

2.5.2 Prejudice Eradication

✧ Exercise

Introduction:

From the introduction of social psychology, you must have understood that an individual behaves differently with a different set of people and also in different circumstances. Many of the social interactions are on individual levels; hence obviously our behavior in the social context is also different. If you try to observe your behavior from a neutral perspective, some of the actions will keep you puzzled. You may introspect and ask why did I behave that way? Why did I help someone? Am I special as a human being? How do I decide to maintain a friendship? Which is more important- personality or the environment? Is there any benefit of living in a group? Does media influence your thoughts? To answer such questions we must learn the way we process the information coming from the world around us. This chapter focuses on individual-level processes.

2.1 Difference between Social Cognition and Social Perception

Social cognition is a broad term used to describe cognitive processes related to perception, understanding, and implementation of linguistics, auditory, visual, and physical cues that communicate emotional and interpersonal information (Suchy, Y. and Holdnack J. A.). While social perception is a study of understanding another person in their social world. It allows individuals to make judgements and impressions about other people.

2.1.1 Social Cognition

If you hear an alarm of fire extinguisher vehicle passing by your road, you rush to the window to see where it is going. Why do you do this? Are you concerned for your safety? Probably yes. Are you worried about people who are in danger? May be. Or just out of curiosity? Most likely. Social cognition helps to understand our ability to reason and to process information about the causes of events. It is one of the most important topics from social psychology which focuses on how people process, store and relate information about other people and social circumstances. It also studies the role of various cognitive processes in social interactions. Simply it can be said that social cognition means understanding the social world. The definitions are as follows-

- The study of mental processes involved in perceiving, attending to and remembering, thinking about, and making sense of the people in our social world" - **Moscowitz, (2005).**
- Social cognition is the sub-topic of psychology that focuses on how people process, store, and apply information about other people and social situations. - **Kendra Cherry, (2019).**

Social cognition explores how people make judgments, form inferences from social information and their own experiences in a social setting. Many times the information available is incomplete, unclear, or even sometimes contradictory. Still, people come to quite a logical conclusion. While making decisions, drawing inferences in a social context we process a huge amount of diverse types of information. While processing the information about the world around us, we take the help of cognitive structures - 'schemas' and mental shortcuts – cognitive heuristics.

1. Schemas:

These are the organized packets of information stored in the long term memory. They describe the pattern of thoughts or behavior which organizes categories of information and the relationship between them. They are mental concepts or mental structures that people use to classify knowledge and guide behavior. Schemas are also used to sort out objects and events to interpret and predict. Schemas make information processing more efficient and faster. It also helps to fill in the gaps of information if any. For example, if someone says to you that he is going to bank for withdrawal. Then you understand that the bank is not the bank of the river, because money transactions are made at the bank which provides financial services.

Many times schemas are influenced by social roles, priorities, primacy (initial impression to interpret information) and individual differences. Sometimes people choose to rely on evidence than their schemas; especially when they need to make an important decision. For example, if a person is having the schema that women are not able to handle office efficiently, then before giving any responsibility to his female coworker, instead of believing his schema he will try to find the abilities of that lady.

Schemas not only help people to form opinions and make decisions, but also tell about the formalities and guidelines while interacting with others.

There are various types of schemas. Few of these include role schema, self-schemas, person schemas, and event schemas. Role schemas are based on typical behavior in a given situation. For example, the role of a doctor, a mother or a teacher. Self-schemas are about the knowledge we are having about ourselves. It includes our ideas about our true self and ideal self. Person schemas focus on particular individuals. What expectations we associate with a certain type of person. For example, your schema for a sociable person might include information about her appearance, her behaviors, her personality, etc. The event schemas focus on the patterns of behavior that should be followed for certain events. It is like a script informing you of what you should do, how you should act, and what you should say in a particular situation. For example, if your teacher enters the classroom all are expected to stand and show respect. It also includes general knowledge about how people behave in certain social situations. For example, if anyone says, "Hi, how are you?" Then in reply you say, "I am fine, Thank you."

2. Cognitive Heuristics:

These are one of those strategies which aid in making decisions faster. We make hundreds of decisions every day. What to eat for breakfast, whether to reply to the message on the phone or not, whether to study or watch a movie and so on. When we come across any situation or any person usually we are overloaded with information. We have to manage our thoughts and behavior from the rapid and complex flow of information in the social world. Cognitive heuristics help to reduce complex or confusing information to more clear. It is a mental shortcut that allows us to solve problems and make judgements quickly and efficiently. It helps us to think through the possible outcomes quickly and arrive at a solution. There are various types of heuristics. Some of them include availability heuristics, representative heuristics and affect heuristics.

Availability heuristics are based on the information which is available to the mind at that particular moment. We make judgements about the possibility of an event based on how easily any example, instance, or case comes to our mind. In this type, a decision-maker relies upon the knowledge that is readily available rather than examine another alternative. Sometimes it may not be valid. It is a basic short cut. For example, if a person reads news of the plane crash, then while booking his tickets to go outstation, he may choose to go by train than flight, even if the train accidents might be more in number!

Fig. 2.1: Use of availability heuristics

The representative heuristics focuses on a comparison between the current situation and the most representative mental image. For example, if you meet a delightful old lady, remembering your grandmother you assume that old lady as kind. If you see a person jogging and having a protein shake, you consider him or her as health-conscious because the description matches your representation for a fitness freak.

The affect heuristic is also one of the influential heuristics in decision making or sorting out the information. Our choices strongly get affected by the emotions we are experiencing at that moment. For example, an angry person is more likely to blame individuals than circumstances. Or if a person is in a positive emotional state, he is more likely to make out an activity which has high benefits and low risks.

Heuristics can also contribute to things such as stereotypes and unfairness. While using these mental shortcuts to classify and categorize people, we may ignore more relevant information. Hence while making inferences and important decisions one must be aware of both sides of the heuristics.

2.1.2 Social Perception

Social perception allows people to understand other people in their social world. In our daily routine, we come across so many situations where we hear people saying," I understand !" But it is one of the complex and difficult tasks. When a father scolds his child for not getting good marks in the exam, does he understand him? When you refuge rudely any beggar at the traffic signal, do you understand him? It is not easy to understand others easily.

Social perception simply means the perception of social processes. It takes place in a social situation where two or more people interact with each other and perceive each other's behavior in social situations.

Social perception is the study of how people form impressions of and make inferences about other people as independent personalities. Simply it is a process through which we seek to know and understand people. Other people play a significant role in our lives to such an extent that we keep ourselves engaged in thinking that what will be their opinion, how they will react or behave in a certain situation, what impression they are carrying? Whether I will be liked by them or not and so on. Social perception study focuses on four aspects namely, non-verbal communication, attribution, nature of impression formation and accuracy.

1. Non-verbal Communication:

It is one of the most influential ways of communication. It is the communication between individuals that does not involve the content of spoken language. In this type of communication, messages are sent or received without words, either written or spoken. It relies on facial expressions, touch, eye contact, and body language with which social perception is facilitated.

According to Dr. Albert Mehrabian research findings, the speech is conveyed in 7%-38%-55% proportions; where **words** account for 7%, **tone of voice** accounts for 38% of the meaning, and **body language** accounts for 55% of the total.

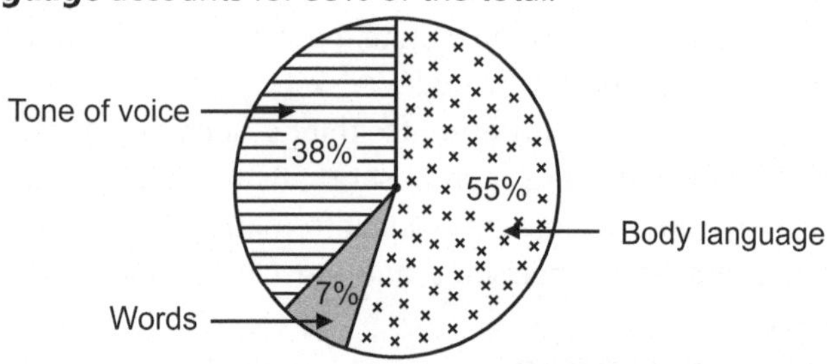

Fig. 2.2: Dr. Mehrabian's 7%-38%-55% rule of communication

People form impressions of others very quickly based on minimum information obtained from the body language and other non-verbal ways of communication.

Generally, people pay attention to the unusual or distinctive qualities of others. More often the information about others is gathered from their facial expressions, eye contact, physical appearance, proxemics, etc.

From walking style to standing style, from fashion sense to hair cut, non-verbal details reveal personality to some extent. Facial expressions are responsible for a large proportion of non-verbal communication. Face and eyes express the secret of the mind. It was found in one of the studies that bronze medalists smile more than the silver medalist. Bronze medalists are happy to grab at least one of the medals. But silver medalists are unhappy as they missed gold.

Whatsapp emojis can be given as a perfect example, where a face even without a nose can express various emotions and feelings quite accurately.

Fig. 2.3: Whatsapp emojis conveying various feelings

Few of the facial expressions such as smile, frowning, tearful eyes, and disgust are universal. It means joy, sadness, and aversion is expressed in the same manner throughout the world. On the contrary, few of the facial expressions are culture-specific. Raising an eyebrow, biting or chewing of lips, rolling of eyes, intense eye contact and many more; each action conveys something without words to another person. Not only face, but the whole body also conveys many things about a person; for example, arms folded in front of the body, sitting slumped with head downcast and so on.

2. Attribution- Understanding the Cause of Other's Behavior:

Sometimes you must have got an experience where you were surprised to observe your friend's weird behavior. You simply didn't understand the reason. Probably that time you didn't want to know *how* he has acted, but wanted to know *why*? Attribution helps to understand the reason or cause behind others' behavior. The cause of the behavior, can be assigned to internal or external factors. According to Baron and Byrne, attribution is the process through which we seek to identify the causes of others' behavior and so gain knowledge of their stable traits and dispositions. As per correspondent inference theory which is given by Jones and David, while understanding the cause of behavior, people pay attention to intentional behavior than an accidental one. This theory describes how we use others' behavior as a basis for inferring their stable disposition. For example, if your friend is behaving aggressively, then you give the reason that he is an aggressive person. If your friend keeps you waiting at the movie, you say he is always non-punctual. It means we draw correspondent inferences from their behavior.

Another theory that explains attribution is Kelley's theory of causal attributions which talks about internal and external factors. The cause of the behavior could be internal like a person's traits, motives or intentions. For example, a person is laughing while watching a comedy show because he is the kind of person who laughs a lot. Or, the cause of behavior could be external which are because of the situation or other environmental aspects. For example, a person is laughing while watching a comedy show because the comedian is very funny.

According to Kelley, to find out 'why' of any behavior, we consider three dimensions such as consensus, consistency and distinctiveness which describe agreement, stability or regularity and uniqueness of the behavior, respectively.

The consensus is the extent to which others behave in the same way towards the stimuli or events in a similar situation.

Consistency is the extent to which the person always behaves the same way towards the stimuli every time the situation occurs.

And distinctiveness is the extent to which the person responds in the same manner to other different stimuli or events.

To understand these three dimensions let us have an example – Ram is a boy who is present as an audience in a comedy show, and he is laughing.

(i) Consensus: If everyone in the audience is laughing, consensus is high and no one other; but only Ram is laughing, consensus is low.

(ii) Consistency: If Ram always laughs at this particular comedian, then consistency is high; but if Ram rarely laughs at this comedian, then consistency is low.

(iii) Distinctiveness: If Ram laughs only at this comedian, then distinctiveness is high and if Ram laughs at every other comedian, then distinctiveness is low.

Thus, with the help of various theories from social perception, and applying that knowledge to your life incidences, you can better understand the causes of the behavior of others.

3. Nature of Impression Formation- Combine and Use Social Information:

It is always said that the first impression is the last. Does it matter really? Probably yes! The moment we look at any unfamiliar person, the process of impression formation starts, though we are not aware of this, we end up either forming a positive or negative impression about that person. We look at a person and immediately a certain impression of his character forms itself before us.

We have seen the previous section that aspects of social perception, such as non-verbal communication, attribution require a lot of hard work. But it is also not always easy to have inferences about others' behavior using these aspects. In contrast, forming first impression seems to be relatively effortless. How do we form a combined impression about another person in a relatively quick and effortless way?

Solomon Asch - a pioneer in the study of impression formation - suggested that we do not form impressions simply by adding together all the traits we observe in other persons. Rather we perceive these traits concerning one another so that the traits end to exist individually and become a part of an integrated dynamic whole.

It is also considered as the first impression lasts longer. To make good impressions, other individuals often are busy in impression management. This can be achieved in following two ways:

(i) Self-enhancement: where people take efforts to boost one's appeal. For example, women use eye makeup, put lipstick to color their lips to enhance their look. They also use attractive accessories and other ways so that they can have a good and long-lasting impression on others. Males also make a styled beard, haircut so that they get an eye-catching look.

Along with these people also use other techniques to impress others by their personality such as talking about self.

Fig. 2.4: Self-enhancement by having different haircut and beard

(ii) Another enhancement: Another way of impression formation is another enhancement in which efforts are made to bring a positive mood into others. For example, soothing others, taking interest in others' work, helping them, etc.

4. Accuracy of Social Perception:

Many times we get encountered with inconsistent non-verbal cues, we make errors in attributions and also sometimes become unable to integrate all the observable traits of other person and ultimately we fail to understand others. In spite of complexity, inadequacy, and intrigue in information regarding people and the social world; we become successful in forming quite an accurate perception of others and events.

To summarize, it can be said that to have a better understanding of another person, if we analyze the way we process information from the social world, observe non-verbal cues coming from others and try to find causes behind others' behavior; we can better deal intrapersonal and interpersonal relations.

2.2 Self-Concept

From your childhood days, somebody must have asked a question, "Who are you?" That time you must have answered, "I am a boy, or girl or son or daughter, or student". You also say "this is my house, this is my hand, this is my college, or this is my nation", etc. But what makes you 'you'? When and how we understand the concept of self?

Self-concept is our knowledge of who we are. The knowledge comprises all of our thoughts and feelings about ourselves physically, personally, and socially. It also includes our knowledge of how we behave, what are our capabilities, and own characteristics. Simply it can be said, self-concept is a perception or idea one is having about self which the person has acquired from evaluation of self.

Social psychologist Roy Baumeister studied how we think about the self, and why we feel and act the way we do.

2.2.1 Definitions of Self-concept

- Self-concept is the individual's belief about himself or herself, including the person's attributes and who and what the self is. **- R. Baumeister (1999).**
- It is the totality of an individual's thoughts and feelings having reference to himself as an object. **- Rosenberg (1979).**

- The self-concept can best be viewed as a theory that a person holds about himself as an experiencing, functioning being in interaction with the world. - **Epstein (1973).**
- The phenomenal self includes all those parts of the phenomenal field which the individual experiences as part or characteristic of himself. - **Snygg and Combs (1949) .**

Fig. 2.5: Girl developing a sense of self

2.2.2 Nature

Before understanding the nature of self-concept, let's know the difference between self and self-concept. In social psychology, the self is referred to as a *process*; and the self-concept, on the other hand, is considered as a *product*. The development of self-concept is related to several other constructs such as self-image, self-esteem, self-efficacy, etc.

As the self is referred to as a process, it remains dynamic throughout life. Consequently, the self-concept, which is the product, keeps changing its form. Thus it can be said that self-concept is malleable. Though our self-concept starts developing during early childhood, it continues to change with age.

In the previous semester, while studying personality we have studied that no two personalities are repeated. Everyone is unique. The self which is specific to every person has been different. Self-concept gets developed as per the need, motivation, attitude, and temperament of the person. Hence self-concept is subjective. Similarly, after every experience, usually, we introspect or analyze our thoughts and behavior. This metacognition i.e. thinking about thinking helps in bringing changes in the self-concept. These changes ultimately shape personality. Hence self-concept may be considered as a core of personality. For example, if a person consistently gets negative experiences, and his evaluation about self is unconstructive as well, then there are high chances that his personality also turns pessimist.

2.2.3 Self-Regulation

Do you remember you decided to study systematically from the very first day of this semester or exercise regularly as you see increased digits on the weighing machine or have a habit of reading the newspaper every day? But somehow you become unsuccessful to do it. But there are some of you and many other people who complete the task they have decided. Once they commit to themselves, then they strictly follow that.

Students, there are many things we decide to do or not to do. Initially for a few days, we certainly follow that decision, but eventually most of the time we give up and return to the earlier habit.

When you decide to lose weight, then you should say no to junk food your friend is offering. But you may control yourself and get tempted to eat. It means you were unable to regulate your behavior.

Fig. 2.6: Why he is choosing to sit, eat and not exercise?

Self-regulation refers to our ability to direct our actions and control our desire so that we achieve our target. It involves being able to set goals, monitor own behavior to make sure that the behavior is in line with those goals, and having the determination to continue until goals are reached. Self-regulations can be simply defined as control of oneself by oneself.

Why people behave the way they do? Why did people choose to do a one activity over another? Why does one person continue even in difficulty, while another person withdraws and gives up? Many situations of life need opposition to situational pressures and control over ourselves.

People who can change their thinking and behavior according to the demands of the external environment are high on self-regulation. For delaying or deferring the gratification of needs is called self-control. It was seen that self-control or self-regulation plays a significant role in the fulfilling of long term goals.

According to modern Self Regulation Theory expert Roy Baumeister, there are four components involved (2007): Standards of desirable behavior; Motivation to meet standards; Monitoring of situations and thoughts that precede breaking standards; allowing one's internal strength to control urges. Allen Bandura, an expert on self-efficacy, said that self-regulation is an active process, where one monitors, judges and reacts to their behavior.

Considering the expectations (that we and others have from ourselves) and taking the situation into account the right and desired change in behavior is termed as self-regulation.

When people try to regulate their behavior means they are deciding to respond to one of the many stimuli. Self-regulation means giving importance to one of the stimuli to respond.

Thus self-regulation is subjective. Because which activity to choose, which stimulus to respond is decided as per the motivation, attitude, beliefs, and morals of the person. In other words, it can be said that self-regulation is conscious personal management that helps the person to think or act. It is not compliance which refers to changing one's behavior due to the request or direction of another person. Probably, now you must have understood why you study whenever *you* want to study and not when your mother says you to study.

Factors Affecting Self-regulation:

There are various strategies as well as factors that are responsible for self-regulation. According to Bandura, people use both reactive and proactive strategies to regulate their behavior. People reactively attempt to reduce the gap between accomplishment and goals, and they proactively set newer and higher goals.

While regulating one's behavior along with external factors, internal factors as well show great influence. It means the behavior is explained as being shaped and controlled by environmental influences or driven by internal dispositions. External factors affecting self-regulation include societal standards and external reinforcement. Societal standards are such as getting good rank in the college exam. External reinforcement helps to regulate self behavior of those people who are not satisfied with internal rewards. For example, if a person is hoping for his promotion or raise in salary, he will work hard; will participate in workplace activities, etc. Internal factors which affect self-regulation are persons' attitude, interest, beliefs, and sense of right and wrong.

As per Bandura, internal requirements for self-regulation comprises of self-observation, judgemental process, and self reaction. Thus people must monitor own performance and have awareness of what they are doing. They must also judge their performance according to goals, personal standards, and evaluate that success is due to own efforts. Self reaction means a positive and negative response to the behavior.

Self-regulation helps a person to adapt and make fine changes as per the situation and need.

2.2.4 Self-Presentation

The self-concept of a person seems to be quite personal and private as what he thinks about himself is hidden and not observable. But the social side of a person is hightly observable as it is the way he presents himself in front of society. It is his 'self-presentation'.

Everyone wants to present a desired image of self to both; an external audience (other people) and an internal audience (ourselves) as well. Thus self-presentational behavior is any behavior that is intended to create, modify, or maintain a person's impression in the minds of others because being a social entity, we have more concern about others. Therefore, self-presentation can be considered as an attempt to lead people to think of ourselves in a particular way. It refers to how people try to present themselves to control how others view them. People get engaged in self-presentation means they are involved in expressing themselves and behaving in ways that create the desired impression. With the help of self-presentation, we can impress society.

Definitions of Self-presentation:

- "The tendency of an individual to put a good image of him before the world." - **Mayors (1999).**
- "It is one of the techniques for creating the effective influence of oneself in the minds of others". - **Jones and Pittman (1982).**

Factors Influencing Self-presentation:

The factors determining the choice of self-presentation can be divided into three basic groups: Individual personal factors, Inter-individual factors, and Situational factors of the social environment. Personal factors are one of the basic sources of presentation dynamics. They include self-confidence, self-consciousness, extraversion, self-esteem, perceived self-efficiency, social anxiety, and the impact of personal experiences.

Along with these few capabilities, good communication skills, self-regulation skills, and social perception skills are also significant.

Few more personal factors involved in self-presentation are false modesty and self-defensive approach. For example, few people try to be exorbitantly humble and submissive, but sometimes they can be mistakenly assumed to be less confident. Some people are always busy in defending their behaviors or their failures by giving excuses and justifications. They mostly perform any job given to them with substandard quality; so that no one keeps expectations from them later. But these ways are proved as obstacles in their growth.

Interpersonal factors may be conditionally attributed to the outside factors, which influence the self-presentation motivation, the choice of strategies, etc. Interaction between the expectation of self-presenting people and audience; quality and significance of other people, the behavior of other people, etc. include inter-individual factors while deciding self-presentation strategy.

Situational factors determining the choice of self-presentation can be represented by public conditions, limitations of social role, the value of the goal attained by self-presentation, feedback from society, etc.

Thus the self-presentation motivation and behavior in public social surrounding is influenced by many such connected and interdependent internal and external factors.

2.3 Attitude (Evaluating Social World)

Generally, attitude is defined as the tendency to evaluate virtually anything in the world in a certain way. It may include the evaluation of people, events, objects, ideas, or issues. It is the extent to which one forms either favorable or unfavorable reaction towards that particular thing. Consider, you have seen an intelligent student of your class copying during the exam. Or you have always seen your parents as loving, caring and very supportive. Such experiences help you to form your attitude towards friend and parents respectively.

In social psychology, attitudes are researched and studied more because though not always, but often they do affect a person's behavior. For example, if a person is having negative attitude towards working women, then he may not allow his sister, wife or daughter to do a job. Or if you have a negative attitude towards the current government, during the election you may avoid voting. Similarly, if you hold a positive attitude towards celebration and hotelling, then it will be seen frequently in your behavior. Why a person holds an extreme attitude which even permits him to kill someone. Why do people ask for a hunger strike putting their life in danger?

Why people have either a positive or negative attitude? How are these attitudes formed? Once formed, attitudes usually are difficult to change. As people's attitude eventually will be going to be an attitude of society, to build useful and positive attitudes has become the need. Because though attitudes are enduring, they can also change.

2.3.1 Definitions

Social psychologists and sociologists have defined attitude in the following manner.

- An attitude is a positive or negative evaluation of an object which influences human behavior towards that object. - **Micheal Hogg.**
- An attitude is a learned predisposition to respond favorably or unfavorably towards people, an object, an idea, or a situation. - **Martin Fishbein.**
- A mental and neural state of readiness, organized through experience, exerting a directive or dynamic influence upon an individual's response to all objects and situations with which it is related. - **Allport (1935).**

When we come across different people, ideas, things, and situations; we form either a negative or positive view of them in our minds. This first view formation is as per the previous experience of a similar thing, or it may be based upon our values, or it may be a general opinion about the same. For example, if you have read that walking every day benefits your health, then exercising or walking daily has formed a positive attitude in your mind. Different people may have a different attitude towards the same thing. For example, you may think the use of the internet in early childhood is dangerous, but your friend may think to allow using the internet since early childhood helps children to understand things better. From these examples, you may easily guess that in the first example, attitude towards walking will reflect in your behavior. You will opt to go for a walk or exercise daily. Similarly, in the second example, you will hesitate to allow your younger brother or sister to use the internet, but your friend may not.

Experts have classified attitudes in various groups such as theoretical, economic, aesthetic, social, religious, and political.

2.3.2 Components of Attitude

Psychologists Rosenberg, Eagley and Hovland have given a three-component model of attitude called CAB model. It tells that three major components show a great impact on the formation of attitude. They are – cognitive component, affective component and behavioral component.

1. The Cognitive Component:

The cognitive component of attitude studies one's thoughts and beliefs about any person, idea, or event. It is the way of dealing with information that includes perception, thinking, and memory. Attitudes are formed on how we perceive certain information and how much that information is useful to us. Whenever we think about any person, task, event, or any idea, we think or remember it either as easy or difficult, complex or simple, useful or harmful. This kind of thinking pattern helps to form an attitude about that specific thing. For example, if you frequently get unsatisfied service from any bank, then you form a negative attitude towards that. If you find any person very helping, you have a positive attitude for him.

While booking a vehicle from any cab center, if you find the online booking process tedious, try to shift to some other service provider.

2. The Affective Component:

The affective component includes various emotions and feelings towards any person, object or situation. Have you ever thought to buy any product just because an attractive model says it to buy? Have you changed your opinion regarding any political issue after listening to a speech given by a strong leader? Have you changed your mind from doing or not doing something because your friend has convinced you effectively?

Emotions many times are used as a driving force while building attitude. Various social media content, advertisements, powerful speeches, and other persuasive information or communication do influence our emotional state. Such affective strategies are used to change our attitude.

Fig. 2.7: Effective message which addresses you fear

Our own emotions as well as emotions and facial expressions of others can influence us and can be the determining factor in forming our attitude. The information which appeals to our senses such as good music, attractive face, refreshing aroma, etc. succeeds in their persuasive communication. Whether we feel happy, good, energetic, encouraged, and comfortable or we feel fearful, lethargic, disgusted, or discouraged matter a lot while forming any attitude; in fact, several such emotions play a critical role in the formation of our attitudes.

Inducing fear about certain things is one of the ways of changing the attitude of people. Some messages which talk about don'ts of certain things like safety rules on traffic address your emotion like fear.

3. The Behavioral Component:

The behavioral component of attitude formation is usually dealt with the tendency of people to behave towards the object in a certain way i.e. how the individual acts towards any person, or situation, or idea. People are more likely to behave as per their attitude, which has been formed as a result of personal experience. For example, you may have cast either positive or negative attitude towards reservation policy in India based on whether you get benefited or not by the same.

The behavioral component is the combination of thinking and feeling in a certain way which leads us to act towards it. If we consider any person's company enjoyable (affective component) and think whether he is useful or not (the cognitive component), we form either a positive or negative attitude towards him.

Similarly if consider any sports game to play, to have a positive attitude towards it, it must be enjoyable as well as useful.

According to the cognitive dissonance theory proposed by Leon Festinger in 1975 people prefer their attitudes to be consistent with their behavior. For example, if a person who smokes and aware of its health hazards is going through two contradictory things. To avoid cognitive dissonance he has to either quit smoking or convince himself by keeping the attitude that the negative health effects have been overestimated.

Attitudes do not form in minutes. It takes a longer time to form an attitude towards anything. Many factors such as cultural, environmental, social media, political conditions, societal and family aspects contribute to the formation of attitude.

2.3.3 Dimensions and Formation of Attitude

(A) Dimensions of Attitude:

As attitudes are subjective, they differ from person to person. Thus, even if two persons show the same attitude towards a certain thing, they differ in a few dimensions. People show differences in holding attitudes in these three aspects. Researchers suggest that there are three dimensions of attitude. They are strength, accessibility, and ambivalence.

1. **Strength of Attitude:** It indicates how strongly people hold any attitude. It is the extent to which the attitude is personally relevant to the individual who holds it. The strength of attitude is the extremity or intensity of an attitude. Thus it may be different with different people. Those attitudes which are important to people, or when people have an interest in them tend to be strong. Strong attitudes are ones that are firmly held (resistant to change) and durable over time, and that has a powerful impact on behavior.

People tend to have stronger attitudes about things, events, ideas, or people they have considerable knowledge and information about those. Strength can be towards positive as well as negative attitudes. For example, if a person holds this attitude that he must have a male child, then the strength of this attitude is so immense that he doesn't mind aborting the female fetus.

Similarly, if an environmentalist has a strong attitude towards conservation of trees, then he may go for *"chipko andolan"* to protect them.

Fig. 2.8

2. Accessibility of Attitude: The accessibility of an attitude refers to the ease with which it comes to mind. The attitude which is formed based on direct experience often exert stronger effects on behavior. Attitudes formed based on direct experience are easy to access i.e. are easier to bring to mind than of those which are formed from indirect ways. Such easily accessible attitudes show a greater impact on behavior. Accessibility of an attitude refers to how often one thinks about it and how quickly it comes to mind. For example, if asked to students that for evaluation, whether internal marking should be applied or not? Then, those students who think a good impression help in getting more marks; show the positive response for internal marking policy, while those who think they are not able to show such flaunting behavior may oppose this policy. (Of course, one must keep in mind that students' evaluation is not dependent on such superficial behavior of students.) In general, attitudes which are highly easily available or accessible tend to be stronger.

3. Ambivalence of Attitude: Ambivalence of an attitude refers to the fact that evaluations of objects, issues, people or events are not always uniformly positive or negative, rather it is mostly mixed. It is the ratio of positive and negative evaluations that make up that attitude. The ambivalence of an attitude increases as the positive and negative evaluations get more and more equal. Ambivalent attitudes are conflicted evaluations that include both positive and negative feelings about an object of thought. It increases as the ratio of positive to negative evaluations get closer to being equal. For example, a girl likes ice cream shows a positive attitude towards it. But still, she doesn't eat it. This can be because of the negative evaluation of ice cream as it is responsible for making her fat. Thus, liking ice cream and not eating it indicates the third aspect of attitude – ambivalence. Whenever there will be a shift towards either positive or negative evaluation, ambivalence will diminish.

2.3.4 Attitude Formation

Attitudes are not inherited. Nor they are formed with a single experience. Rather their formation is a continuous process. Since birth, every individual is exposed to either directly or indirectly numerous stimuli of the environment. Those experiences teach him to develop some ideas, opinions, or certain beliefs towards the same. Attitudes are all those beliefs, feelings, and actions tendencies of an individual or a group of individuals towards object, idea or people. Thus attitude formation depends upon persons' thinking towards any object or other person and upon what experiences he or she had about the same. Attitude formation is a multidimensional and complex process. A few factors influencing attitude are social factors, direct instructions, family values, prejudices, media, educational and religious institutions, economic status, occupation, etc.

Attitudes are also formed by the process of socialization. While interacting with society, the individuals learn about good or bad thoughts, do's and don'ts about certain actions, and the societal norms. also about actions which are rewarded and which are punished. Accordingly, he develops either a positive or negative attitude towards a particular thing. Thus obviously, family values, the behavior of parents, attitudes of an educational institution play a very crucial role in developing an attitude in the child. Along with these, cultural influences, friends, media, relatives, neighbors as well have a big share in the attitude development of an individual.

Research studies reveal that we tend to develop a favorable attitude towards things that help us to satisfy our needs.

There are three major processes of learning which affect the formation of attitudes, they are classical conditioning, instrumental, or operant, conditioning, and observational learning.

1. Classical Conditioning: Learning through classical conditioning is a mere association of unconditioned stimuli with conditioned stimuli to attain conditioned response. For example, a child sees his mother becoming happy after listening to the news of her father visiting their home or father getting irritated after knowing that he has to pay more tax this month. With these experiences, the child learns to associate emotions like happiness or irritation with the arrival of his grandfather and paying the tax respectively. These two situations and the emotions associated with each help the child to form the positive and negative attitudes accordingly. This is an example of classical conditioning. When two stimuli are repeatedly associated, the child learns to respond to them with a similar emotional reaction. When we find our favorite actor or actress telling about a certain product, we form a positive attitude towards it. The government is also using a similar strategy while delivering important messages like polio vaccination, making use of toilets, etc. by using influential personalities in the advertisement.

2. Instrumental or Operant Conditioning: When the behavior is followed by either positive consequence or negative consequence, then accordingly attitudes take shape. According to this theory of learning, we gain knowledge of those responses that are rewarded and show an increased probability of repeating such responses. However, we tend not to repeat responses that are punished. Studies reveal that children develop attitudes maintained by their parents simply because holding such attitudes is rewarding. For example, if unknowingly a child brings any belonging of his friend, then his mother scolds him for this behavior. Associating between action and punishment, the child develops a negative attitude towards stealing. On the contrary, if the child gets praise for helping some elderly person on the road, then the child forms a positive attitude towards altruism.

3. Observational Learning: Since childhood, we have learned several things just by observing the behavior of parents, teachers. Which behavior to continue or which thought to cultivate is decided after observing the outcome of the same. Most of the times children follow a similar thought pattern of their parents or teachers without questioning, only because they trust in the wisdom of parents and significant other members of society. But, after a certain age, when the child gets exposed to a bigger world, their attitudes may remain the same or even may change depending on how strong the earlier attitude was. For example, when a child sees his mother serving tea for the guests, by frequent observation of this gesture, he also learns to develop a positive attitude of hospitality.

Along with such learning and observational methods we form our attitudes. Once formed, usually, attitudes are difficult to change. But with the help of persuasion and various theoretical orientations such as functional, consistency, learning, dissonance and perceptual approach attitudes can be changed. Characteristics of existing attitude, credibility and attractiveness of source of new information, motive, and importance of new information and characteristics such as intelligence, the self-esteem of the target person, etc. are significant factors in attitude change.

2.4 Prejudice

Prejudice means prejudgment. A person is said to be prejudiced when he forms an attitude towards a particular idea, thing, group, or person before having enough information to form a knowledge-based opinion. Prejudices are examples of attitudes towards a particular group. They are unjustified or incorrect attitude (usually negative), may be based on stereotypes about the specific group. For example, a person who is prejudiced towards some community or race tends to evaluate its members negatively just because they belong to that community or race. A negative prejudice is that when the attitude is unreceptive towards members of a group and a positive prejudice is the unduly favorable attitude towards a group. For example, all political leaders are corrupt or all women are very loving and caring.

Prejudices may be for any of the following characteristics such as religion, ethnicity, language, gender, age, social class, or even skin color.

"Prejudice is an antipathy based on faulty and inflexible generalization. It may be felt or expressed. It may be directed towards a group or an individual of that group". The classic definition of prejudice is given by the famous Harvard psychologist, Gordon Allport, who published "*The Nature of Prejudice* in 1954".

All prejudices include three i.e. affective, behavioral and cognitive components. Stereotypes about the specific group are the cognitive component of prejudice. This cognitive component is mostly accompanied by dislike or hatred which is the affective component. Prejudice may also get converted into discrimination - the behavioral component of it, whereby people behave in a less positive way towards that specific group. For example, the deliberate killing of Jewish people by the Nazis in Germany can be considered as an extreme example of prejudice that can lead to hatred. Prejudices and discrimination often go together. Discriminatory behavior of people can be lessened by putting rules and regulations, or laws, but, the cognitive and affective component is hard to change.

Prejudice is baseless with the common feature of negative feelings, stereotyped beliefs, and tendency to discrimination against members of that group. In other words, it can be said that people paint every individual with one color and fail to look at each one as a unique. Thus prejudice and stereotypes may be considered as our mental mistakes which are because of our inclination to quickly label people or events in the world around us. For example, labeling all women as awful car drivers, or saying every member of the young generation as irresponsible,etc.

2.4.1 Causes

There are various causes which are responsible to form prejudice. Prejudices are formed as a result of learning from family, media, personal experiences or other reference groups. But why do many people form and hold prejudiced views? According to Steel, Spencer, and Lynch, 1993; people hold prejudices because it strengthens their image. For example, when an American holds a negative attitude towards any black person; then this allows him to confirm his self-worth. Thus by doing this, he feels superior. Holding such a negative view protects or enhances his self-concept.

Fig. 2.9: Holding superiority complex increases prejudice

Prejudice allows us to believe stereotypes because it asks us to work cognitively to a lesser extent and we don't need to work with new information.

Some people believe that prejudice is because of the result of people's desire to feel better.

Others believe prejudice comes from the competition between groups for scarce resources (e.g., food, jobs). Still a few argue that prejudice is an innate human response that developed to protect humans from dangerous strangers.

2.5 Application: Attitude Formation and Prejudice Eradication

How do you feel if you were not allowed to enter to any hotel or any worship place just because of the specific cast, or because of your skin color? Isn't it humiliating? Remember your History studies of pre-independence time. As per that Indians were treated disrespectfully and "Dogs and Indians are not allowed" used to be on notice board at many places. Unfortunately, these scenarios are a reality for many people even today. It represents a negative or hostile attitude towards people because they belong to a specific group or community.

Fig. 2.10: Discrimination against Indians during the pre-independence time

Prejudice is part of human nature, hence it is seen everywhere in the world. Higher cast-lower cast, high socio economic-low socio-economic, etc. are too visible universally. Their side effects are also found all over the world.

For harmonious social interaction and to establish goodwill in the individuals; following are some of the measures that psychologists have suggested to eliminate prejudice.

2.5.1 Attitude Formation

During the process of attitude formation and even after that, attitude modification can be achieved with the help of various influences. As a negative attitude gets transformed into a prejudice which in turn into discriminating behavior, it is recommended to change an attitude so that ultimately discriminating behavior can be diminished. But practically bringing change in the attitude of people is of interest to community leaders, politicians, advertisers, and others. After understanding the process of attitude formation we may be able to work for prejudice eradication. Thus if we want to make positive changes in human beings as well as in society, change in attitude must occur. Though various contradictory attitudes regarding feminism, emancipation, racism, casteism, etc. are becoming obstacles in the growth of society, still people are not open to accept change and modify their attitudes. Because of deep routed prejudices, attitudes are getting rigid. Hence to change attitudes, it is extremely important to eradicate prejudices.

2.5.2 Prejudice Eradication

Following are some of the measures that psychologists have suggested to eliminate prejudice for social interaction and to establish goodwill in the individual. A number of these techniques can be applied at school, workplace, community.

1. **Rejection of Stereotypes:** Avoiding conservative, conventional or rigidly embedded ideas is an effective way to eliminate prejudice. Each person as an independent person, treating them with equality, judging every member of any specific group with biased thoughts may result in the elimination of prejudice.
2. **Contact and Cooperation:** Contact and cooperation approaches stem from the work of Gordon Allport in the 1950s. He stated the **contact hypothesis**, that interaction between members of conflicting groups reduces the occurrence and intensity of prejudiced beliefs and actions. The idea is that time spent between the groups breaks down the divide between "us" and "them" through positive contact and familiarity with individuals instead of stereotyping groups.

Fig. 2.11: Direct contact helps in reducing prejudice

3. **Recategorization:** There can be another way that will weaken the difference between groups that may be based on gender, ethnicity, caste, race, etc. Recategorization helps people to realize that both groups are part of a larger group uniting them while understanding the difference and respecting each other. Increasing intergroup contact allows for direct communication, removal of mistrust between groups, and even discovering positive qualities in the out-group.
4. **Feelings and Affect:** Emotional methods can be effectively used to reduce prejudice. Teaching empathy, helping people to understand others' perspectives can be taught from early childhood.
5. **Use of Social Media:** All types of social media such as newspapers, television, movies, the internet, etc. can be used very effectively. As they contribute in generating attitudes and prejudice, they can be used to eradicate the same.

Thus, knowing about the causes or sources would be the first step in reducing prejudice. Then using various strategies the process of attitude change and prejudice reduction can be made effective.

Thus using various such strategies, attitude formation and prejudices eradication can be successfully achieved.

✧ Exercise ✧

Q. 1 : Answer the following questions in 100 words :

(1) What is social cognition?

(2) What is meant by self-regulation?

(3) Define self-presentation.

Q. 2 : Answer the following questions in 200 words :

(1) Explain the importance of non-verbal communication in social perception.

(2) Explain in brief the cognitive component of attitude.

(3) What is attribution?

Q. 3 : Answer the following questions in 400 words :

(1) Explain in detail the attitude formation and role of classical conditioning in attitude formation.

(2) Give the concept of cognitive heuristics in detail.

(3) What is the ambivalence of attitude?

Q. 4 : Write short notes :

(1) Nature of impression formation

(2) Self-concept

(3) Prejudice reduction

✧ Questions from Previous University Exams ✧

(1) State the impression management. ***(Oct 2011)***

(2) What is social cognition? ***(April 2012)***

(3) Explain the components of attitudes. ***(April 2016, 2017)***

(4) What is Impact of schemas on social cognition? ***(April 2013)***

(5) Write a note on Self regulation and self representation. ***(April 2013)***

(6) Explain sources of attributional error. ***(May 2014)***

(7) Explain factors in attitude. ***(October 2017)***

☆☆☆

UNIT – 3

Interpersonal Processes

SYNOPSIS

3.1 Introduction

3.1.1 Interpersonal Attraction

3.1.2 Love

3.2 Pro-Social Bahaviour – Helping Others

3.2.1 Increasing Pro-Social Behaviour

3.3 Locus of Control

3.3.1 Internal versus External Control of Reinforcement

3.3.2 Increasing Our Helping Nature

3.4 Aggression

3.4.1 Meaning of Aggression

3.4.2 Nature of Aggression

3.4.3 Causes of Aggression

3.5 Applications: Prevention and Reducing Aggression

3.5.1 Anger Reduction and Punishment

3.5.2 Catharsis

3.5.3 Cognitive Intervention

✧ Exercise

3.1 Introduction

Interpersonal relations started thousands of years ago when since civilizations started. Earlier, all humans lived as hunter-gatherers and were nomadic. With farming and agricultural development near rivers most humans transitioned from a nomadic to a settled lifestyle. This means that since evolution humans have required companionship, love, support, etc. Since then, people have been living with and interacting with family and community in a set system. Relations and other people play a very significant role in our life.

Can you find any moment while awake without anyone in person or virtual? If you post any of your photos on social media and no one gives any comment on it, does this upset you? Do you get bored when alone?

We are used to the company of others to such an extent that we cannot think of enjoying life without people. Constantly, we are engaged in interpersonal interactions; which have begun as soon as we started breathing. Within family and hence in society we are attached with people by means of many relations such as son, daughter, brother, sister, uncle, aunt, grandfather, grandmother, friends, neighbors, teachers, etc. These attachments and attractions further lead into development of relations. Thus, our relations start with our family.

Though we are surrounded by more than 7 billion persons globally, we have very few around our vicinity. But we prefer to have close relationships with still fewer. When you took admission to this college, many of the students were new to you. But after some days, you became more attached to very few amongst all. What forces to choose few over many? Similarly, people who have spend a long time with each other, at some point of life choose to break the relation and prefer to stay without each other.

In this unit we are going to learn what factors are responsible for people to have interpersonal attractions to pursue close relationships.

3.1.1 Interpersonal Attraction

Interpersonal attraction can be defined as the force acting between two people that brings them to form some type of relationship. It is the positive feeling about another person. It is also a desire to approach and get affiliated with other people. It can take on many forms, such as friendship, respect, love, neighborhood, admiration, lust, adoration, etc. Though interpersonal attraction may not explain relationships, it can show how some relationships can be formed. With this knowledge, people can make decisions about how close we get to some people. Theories of interpersonal attractions are used for explaining the choice patterns of peer relations, attachments, etc. There are two main approaches to explain interpersonal attractions; these are the cognitive consistency theory i.e. Balance Theory developed by Heider in 1958 and reinforcement theory which is the Social Exchange Theory developed by Homans in 1951.

1. Balance Theory (Heider, 1958):

Balance theory tells the need to focus on perception of the individual on a relationship instead of focusing on other facts. Heider argued that friendship selections involved every individual's hunt for constancy between attraction feelings for others along with individual's beliefs, outlooks, and values. People go for out for having friendship that creates a balance between the ways they feel and the actions they take. He outlined the scopes with which an individual is attracted such as proximity and reciprocity.

2. Social Exchange Theory (Homans, 1951):

Another approach is reinforcement theories. It is a completely contrasting approach. These theories propose that interpersonal relations are greatly influenced by rewards and punishments in the physical environment. One of the important theories of interpersonal theories was developed by Homans known as Social Exchange Theory. It argues that specific features are appreciated between diverse groups and in the course of interpersonal interactions; a system of costs and benefits is operational. Benefits will be in the form of rewards like love and social acceptance. The benefits motivate the individual to continue the relationship.

Thus interpersonal attractions can be explained on three aspects; cognitive, affective and behavioral. Cognitive aspect consists of beliefs and knowledge about other person, affective part deals with feelings towards other, and behavioral aspect talks about tendencies to either approach or avoid that person. Hence there can be external and internal determinants of interpersonal attraction.

3. External Determinants of Attraction:

(a) Proximity: It is the geographical closeness. It is an obvious and basic requirement for any relationship to form as people involved need to have opportunities to interact with each other. For example, you may love a film-star or a sports person, but you won't be able to form relation with him or her if you never get any chance to meet or talk to them.

Having more chances to interact with another person means to become more familiar with that person. Generally people prefer familiar persons rather than strangers. This is known as 'repeated exposure' or 'mere exposure effect' (Zajonc, 1968). According to this, it is the reason why people are more likely to be attracted to them whom they meet more often. Social psychologists like Theodore Newcomb and Leon Festinger also support the principle of proximity and propinquity. Studies provide confirmation to support the fact that people who come across each other more frequently tend to develop stronger relationships. Physical closeness between two individuals with respect to where they live, or work increases the likelihood that two people will come into repeated contact and exposure to each other, feel positive effect, and develop reciprocal attraction. As per Allyn and Bacon (2006), frequent exposure without harmful effects increases familiarity, reduces uncertainty, and increases liking. But this characteristic of attraction is not always true. Because this effect may not happen if people's initial reaction is negative, otherwise all classmates, colleagues, neighbors, all the friends, etc. may be having attractions with each other. Hence when two people progress towards getting to know each other only if they are motivated to affiliate.

The knowledge from research findings are used by architects to design offices in such a way where more social interaction could be promoted.

(b) Observable characteristics: One of the major determinants of interpersonal attraction is observable external characteristics of the other person. People get attracted towards those who are physically good-looking. Romantic attraction is primarily determined by physical attributes. The saying "first impression is the last impression" works to a great extent in physical attractiveness of a person. Before getting familiar with person's attitude and other attributes, observable characteristics play crucial role in making either positive or negative impression. Walking style, dressing style, facial expressions, facial features, and overall appearance which are the observable characteristics help people to get along more with each other as they are used for instant evaluation of the individual. For example, when we go to any book shop, before reading the content of any book, just after looking at the cover we decide whether to browse the further or not because it creates either positive or negative impression about the same.

Fig. 3.1: Physical appearance is a key factor in attraction

The person who is sociable, talkative, and attractive is assumed to be better. Attractiveness is associated with popularity as well. There are many stereotypes linked with attractive people, for example, beautiful woman may be perceived as materialistic or a tall and masculine person is assumed to be good leader. Body language is one of the factors people use subconsciously to judge other people. A person with confident walking style, active participation in conversations, etc. is considered to be more intelligent. Similarly, people who eat healthy food than junk food are also judged by others as morally superior.

But it was found in researches that such assumptions and judgements may not be always right. A beautiful woman may be self-centered or immoral, a very famous philosopher who may not be attractive as per the so-called social norms but is very intelligent and some of the more handsome males may be smugglers or murderers. Observable characteristics are not always reliable to draw conclusions about personalities.

(c) Similarity-dissimilarity effect: The phrase "birds of a feather flock together" can be used to explain this effect. It means people who like each other or who share same likes-dislikes, interests, values or motivations tend to spend time with other. You must also have observed in your schools or colleges that the friends who hang out together probably like the same things to do. For example, if two of your friends like to learn French language, then both of them will find coaching for the same and join the class. Obviously they are expected to be together more, share their experience and spend time with each other. If some of your friends like football, then they discuss that topic, watch matches on television in a group and hence spend time with each other. This ultimately leads to more exposure and in proximity. People also tend to like others who reciprocate to their likes and dislikes.

4. Internal determinants of interpersonal attraction:

When two or more than two people interact; the interpersonal attraction that occurs is because of few internal determinants also. They are need of affiliation, emotional status, etc.

(a) Need of affiliation: Though people want to be independent, they always want to be affiliated as well. An affiliation is the strength that allows us to join other groups, be adaptive, and take care of others. It is one of the major aspects of group dynamics. Importance of affiliation is one of the major needs in Maslow's Hierarchy of Needs. When we do not get affiliation, acceptance, or inclusion; sadness, anger, or frustration may arise. People in danger or in problem seek for the help more than when in joyous condition. People like to be in association who are experiencing similar negative situation or going through same trauma. The international association "Alcoholics Anonymous" is an example. It is a support group where people who are struggling with alcoholism meet and discuss their problems and attempt to overcome their addiction.

(b) Affect and interpersonal attraction: Positive as well as negative emotional state of a person is one of the deciding factors in positive or negative evaluations of people. Emotional states influence interpersonal attraction. Many of you must have experienced in early school days, that the teacher who praises you is your favorite teacher. And, on the contrary, the one who scolded is the one you dislike. This experience clearly shows that we generate with positive evaluation for them who makes us feel better. Similarly, we evaluate those people negatively who makes us feel sad, angry, and like. Remember your friend consoling you when you were sad, you start liking that friend because he or she helped you to feel better. Also, you may like the person whom you meet when you are in positive mood, and you may reject the person with negative evaluation if you are in negative mood.

Fig. 3.2: A friend in need is a friend indeed

If any person is jovial, cheerful, cracks jokes and keeps the situation happy; his company is liked by all. The association of positive emotions and positive evaluation of any person acts like conditioning which forces us to experience that feeling again. Hence when we have a positive feeling with anyone, we try to meet that person again.

Thus, interpersonal attractions are the result of many external, internal, as well as interactive factors.

3.1.2 Love

This is one of most interesting topics of our life. When people initially get to know each other, there can be some sort of a relationship. It can be just an acquaintance, friendship, love, passion, or simply lust. But the basic principles of social psychology can be used to understand which relationships would last longer. There are many examples where a long-term couple breaks up soon after getting married, in contrast to two strangers who stay committed and bonded for a very long period in their "arranged" marriages. There are friends who are together since their school days, but due to some misunderstanding avoid each other.

The factors that keep people loving and liking each other in long term relationship are similar to some extent as we seen in interpersonal attraction. For example, physical attractiveness, similar interests, proximity, etc.

Love is one of the more universal emotions. Every person in the world is craving for it. It always makes us feel warm, satisfied, and happy. Sometimes it also causes problems in our relationships. Extreme love for the partner makes that person possessive, intense love for children may result in over parenting. Such examples unfortunately result when two people do not understand each other, and hence their relationship may suffer.

To understand the psychology of love and the key to long-lasting relationships we will know various forms or types of love.

American existential psychologist Rollo May had mentioned in his very famous book, 'Love and Will' various types of love such as Sex, Eros, Philia, and Agape which respectively mean lust, savoring (romantic love), affection (brotherly love) and devotion (spiritual love), etc. For example, love between two partners, friends, parents and children and love towards god.

In colloquial terms the word love is considered as a synonym for romance. But the philosopher Plato told that physical attraction or sexual longing is not essential for love. Hence the love which is without any sexual activities is referred to as 'Platonic Love'. Long lasting friendship, people getting married and staying married; families growing together, etc. are the examples of different dimensions of love. It involves liking which means positive evaluation of that specific individual. It also involves closeness, dependency, selfless behavior, companionship, etc.

Following factors may be studied while studying love.

1. Family: The First Relationship:

Every individual takes birth with the name of some relation; a son or a daughter. All interactions with parents, grandparents, caregivers, and other family members have an influence on what child learns about relationships. Children observe the way parents and other people around behave with each other. The pattern of thinking and manner of behavior of family members provide valuable information about how people deal with one another in social situations. Happy and satisfying relationship within a family is associated with empathy, high self esteem, and interpersonal trust.

Fig. 3.3: Happy family is built on mutual trust

Attachment is one of the major and deep enduring bonds that connect parents and children in family. It may not be reciprocal. Mary Ainsworth and John Bowlby have some great works on the attachment between a child and a mother. As per their studies, there are four various attachment styles - secure, insecure avoidant, insecure ambivalent and disorganized attachment.

An affectionate love is seen in siblings where each sibling has experienced warm relation with each parent, and if the parents perceive their marriage positively. Siblings feel close to each other if they can share their opinions, attitudes, experiences, and help each other. When families grow together, the members rely on each other.

2. Relationship beyond Family:

Do you remember your friends who were your classmates in your early school years? If they are still staying in your vicinity or they are still your classmates then probably they are your very close friends. But if now they are not with you, then probably you may not even remember their names. Usually we get in close friendship with our peers when interact with them frequently. For example, Hollywood stars Leonardo DiCaprio and Tobey Maguire, who were childhood friends, have continued their friendship in adulthood as well though sometimes they may be facing professional competition.

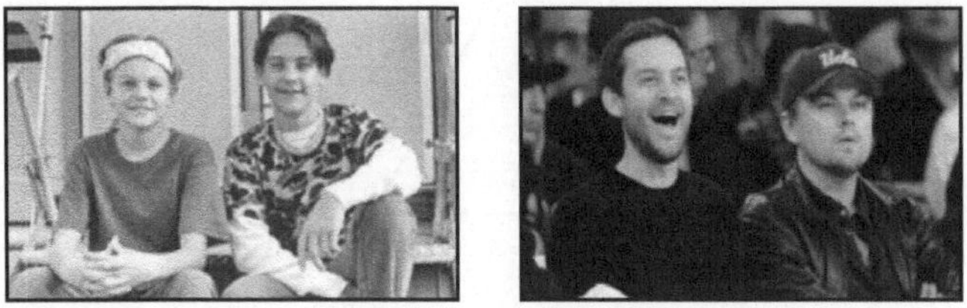

Fig. 3.4: Famous Hollywood stars - childhood friendship

The relationship which we nurture beyond our family tends to consist of mutual liking and positive effect. Generally, friends do not lie to each other. Close friends like to spend time together, interact frequently, and provide emotional support.

3. Gender Specific Friendship:

Is men's friendship different from women's? While spending time with each other what must be the topics of discussion or conversation? The role of gender in relationship and gossip has been researched by psychologists. As per Watson, the gossip may be more of a competitive threat to the relationship in females. While achievement related gossip is related to male friendship quality, which reflects the greater emphasis on individuation in male friendships. It was also noticed that male's friendships tend to be less emotional and based on shared activities, sports, women, etc. While females talk about relationships with men, clothes, personal problems, gifts, etc. Opposite sex friendship study shows interesting findings. Mostly males try to seek physical intimacy. In contrast, females tend to gain physical protection.

4. Triangular Theory of Love:

Dr. Robert J. Sternberg developed a theory called triangular theory of love. This theory can be understood in terms of three components which are vertices of a triangle. The three components are intimacy, passion, and commitment. Intimacy refers to closeness, attachment, and connectedness in relation. The sense of intimacy helps to generate the feeling of satisfaction, acceptance, and warmth, whereas passion deals with romance, physical and sexual attraction. This component includes emotional stimulation, excitement, and enthusiasm. The third component of this theory is the commitment. It involves the conscious decision to remain in the relation even in difficult period of life. One can be committed to a relationship without acknowledging that one loves the other person.

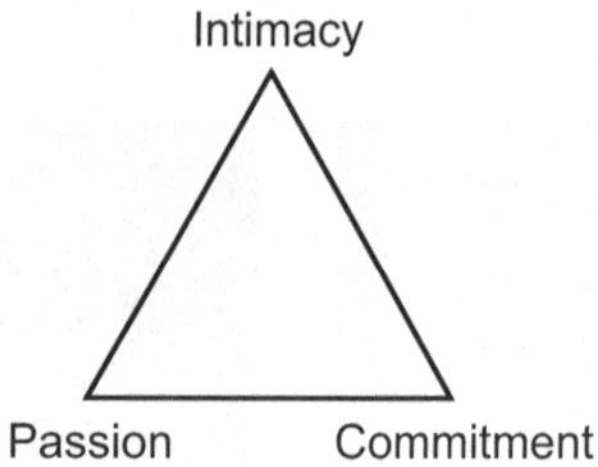

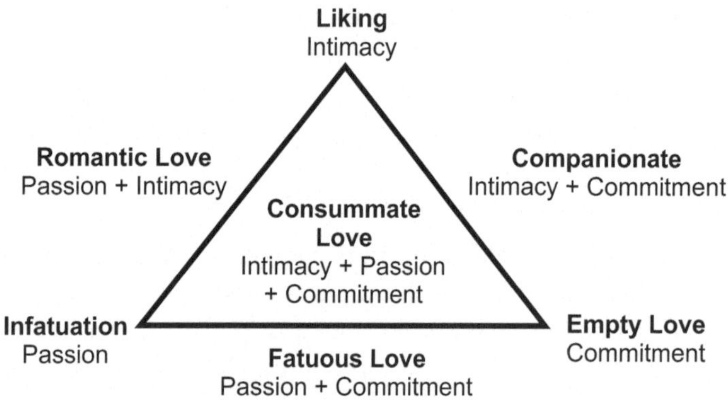

Fig. 3.5: Sternberg's triangular theory of love

As per Sternberg, the combination and interaction of these three components of love generate seven possible kinds of love. As he said, no relationship is likely to have any of these three pure forms. The major aspects of these kinds of love may be summarized as follows.

Friendship is that of love where liking or intimacy is present. Infatuation is characterized by lust and physical attraction. Empty love is commitment without intimacy or passion. Romantic love bonds people emotionally through intimacy and passion. Companionate love is intimate but non-passionate with low or no sexual desire. In fatuous love, commitment and passion are present, at the same time intimacy or liking is absent. The last kind of love, consummate love, is the blend of all. It is the complete form of love. The couples who experience this kind of love enjoy physical intimacy several years. They cannot imagine their lives without each other. They deal with all the differences and stressors together. According to Sternberg, consummate love may be harder to maintain than to achieve it as without behavior and expression, passion is lost, and love may remain as companionate type.

3.2 Pro-Social Behavior - Helping Others

Have you seen anyone helping an elderly person to climb the stairs? Have you ever rushed and helped your teacher to pick up the books that fell from her hands? Also, you must have offered your seat in bus to a lady. This altruistic behavior is termed as pro-social behavior. It is any act that benefits others i.e. the voluntary help to others. This type of behavior is characterized by the action with no immediate benefit to the volunteer. Why do people help others when there is no obvious gain? What are the motives behind such behavior where sometimes there is high risk involved? Whenever there is an emergency, small of big; what makes a person get into pro-social behavior. Let us understand the reasons at the back of these actions.

The study of pro-social behavior among people started in 1964 with a murder on the road. On one evening, a lady named Catherine who was returning from her office was murdered in New York City. When the attacker stabbed her with a knife, she screamed for help. Many lights from the nearby apartment went on, the attacker started to run, but when he noticed nobody was coming to help, he returned and stabbed her to death.

This behavior of bystanders was confusing to psychologists. Why didn't someone help? This question put two social psychologists, John Darley and Bibb Lataneat unrest. They put their well known theory named 'Bystander effect' to explain such behavior. This effect suggests that the presence of others discourages an individual from intervening in an emergency. It means, the chance of helping a person in need is high when the helper is alone than in a group. Usually people prefer to help or take any action in any crisis when there are very few or no witnesses present.

There are few basic factors that influence the chances to decide whether an individual will or will not respond to such situations.

1. Personal Distinctiveness: Everyday experiences show that some people are more pro-social than others. They are able to sympathize with others. In other words, they are skilled in understanding others' thoughts and feelings. Hence they can take others' perspectives. It has been found in studies that these people tend to be positive, well adjusted, and better in expressing their emotions. Such traits can be seen even in early childhood when the children share their toys.

Predispositions, past-experiences, competence, empathy, self interest, moral integrity, and other individual factors are responsible for pro-social behavior.

2. Situational Factors: Many times situations ask people to help others without choice. Peculiarities of the situation have powerful impact. For example, if you are involved in a car accident, then the likelihood that someone will stop and help you decreases if there are many other people present. Because they may assume that because so many other people are present, somebody else will come forward. This decrease in the amount of personal responsibility people feel is known as 'diffusion of responsibility'. Similarly, during such circumstances mostly people look to others in the surrounding to see how they respond. If the situation is somewhat ambiguous, they become less likely to help. Sometimes many people undergo fear of being judged by other members of group. Hence it may happen that someone of the group may initiate the action of help, but fear of being evaluated by others stops him or her to take that action.

Another important effect named pluralistic ignorance is also responsible for people in crowds for not helping the individual in need. Because, none of the bystander in crowd knows for sure what is happening, each depends on the others to furnish information; hence ultimately no one responds. Pluralistic ignorance occurs when people incorrectly infer that they feel differently than peers. Hence often all of the bystanders hold back and behave as if there is no problem. We have also experienced the same many times. When we see someone lying on footpath, we assume he must be a drunk and there is no emergency.

Practically other than diffusion of responsibility and pluralistic ignorance, there are many other factors which influence how people respond. Darley and Latane extended their theory to suggest five key things in order for a person to take action during any emergency. These are:

1. **Noticing the emergency:** Bystanders must first notice and recognize that whatever is happening is not routine, or usual, but it is a problem.

2. **Interpreting the emergency as an emergency:** After noticing the problem, one has to understand and interpret that problem is an emergency and that immediate action is required.
3. **Assuming that it is your responsibility:** The bystander is forced to decide whether he has responsibility to act or not. When a bystander is alone; he or she has the total responsibility during an emergency. But the responsibility gets diffused when there are more onlookers. Similarly, people take responsibility when they are accompanied by a friend.
4. **Knowing what to do:** Though a person understands the problem, the emergency, and assumes the responsibility, it is of no use if the person doesn't know what to do and how to help. For example, if you see a person drowning in the river, you can directly help if you know swimming. But otherwise to ask others to assist and get the proper help can be done.
5. **Making conscious decisions to help:** Though all these previous steps are fulfilled; but the fear of probable difficulties inhibits the person from extending a help. Hence the most important step is the conscious decision to act during the emergency.

3.2.1 Increasing Pro-social Behavior

A commitment to social duty is necessarily an acceptance of the fact that we all are connected to each other and that my deeds and actions have an impact on others. Pro-social behavior, which is the ability of people to act in a positive, accepting, helpful, and supportive approach is linked with well being of an individual and in turn, of the society. Thus, it is very important to inculcate pro-social behavior in children. Though some pro-social skills are in traits of few, they can be even nurtured deliberately. Parents can provide the support to facilitate interpersonal skills among children. They can help children internalize these positive attributes, acknowledge their altruistic behavior and encourage them. Same is true with antisocial behavior. When adults notice and label accordingly, children are better able to understand the difference between right and wrong. Practice and consistency make children able to act in appropriate ways. Few ways to increase pro-social behavior are listed below-

- Modeling is the best way to inculcate pro-social approach in children. 'Walk the talk' method is found to be the best policy in increasing altruism.

- Parents may ask their children to celebrate birthdays in orphanage, old age homes, etc. The habit of sharing is also one of the ways to cultivate empathy.
- Family picnics, treks etc. help children to respect nature. Picking up litter, segregating plastics lying on hills and riverbanks, respecting animals, taking care of natural habitats etc. may be used to teach values and gratitude towards nature.
- Assigning household chores as per their age and capability help them to understand importance of house care. This increases the self esteem and self confidence, which is one of the causes of altruistic behavior.
- Frequent exposure to violent or anti-social behaviors via movies, or any other social media should be avoided as such content may result in lack of empathy.
- Parents should allow children to participate in activities like NSS, NCC, etc. so that they are engaged in social behaviors.

Along with such various ways, children must also be encouraged to grow independently so that they become able to make decisions on their own, solve problem without help, and take responsibility of their behavior.

3.3 Locus of Control

When you pass an examination, do you say it was in my destiny? If you face any failure, do you blame your bad luck? Whatever success you achieve, whether you give credit to your efforts or receive it because of your luck? If you become unsuccessful, do you accept your fewer efforts or blame your destiny? We see many people talking about their life as "I know it is because of me, I have to study more, I must not do this again". Or we also hear people saying, "Nowadays, it is becoming so difficult to face competition, I don't know why God is unfair with me, Why this happens with me only?". It means few people take the responsibility of their life while others say that their life is predestined.

Julian Rotter tried to explain such behavioral difference with the help of thinking patterns of persons.

3.3.1 Internal versus External Control of Reinforcement

In 1966 Rotter published his famous I-E scale to assess the internal and external locus of control. This term was proposed by him which refers to an individual's beliefs about the extent of control they have over things that happen to them. This concept is divided into two categories: Internal (I) and External (E). Internal locus of control is a belief that the reinforcement is brought about by our own behavior, while external locus of control is the belief that reinforcement is under control of external factors such as people, fate, or luck.

Fig. 3.6: Blaming superstitious reason for failure

Rotter developed I-E scale which assesses internal or external locus of control. He found that some people believe that their reinforcers depend on their own efforts, capabilities, and hard work. And they are responsible for their own actions. Other people believe that their reinforcers are controlled by outside world which includes external forces like other people, luck, and destiny. Those who believe in themselves are characterized by internal locus of control, whereas others who think that outside world is responsible for their actions are described as holding external locus of control. People with external locus of control are anyhow convinced that they are dependent on exterior factors.

Hence it can be clearly seen that our locus of control can have a considerable influence of our behavior. Hence, to be motivated, determination, and perseverance for any action or to give up and accept the situation as it depends upon the locus of control of the individual.

Philip Zimbardo in his 1985 book 'Psychology and Life' explained locus of control as the belief about whether the outcome of our actions is contingent on what we do or on events outside our personal control.

People with internal locus of control are more likely to take action to change the adverse situation with hard work, whereas external locus of control think that their abilities make no difference in the outcome so why should they try when they have no control on the external factors. Because a person with external locus of control, who attributes his or her success to luck or fate, will be less likely to take pains to change or get control over any situation. On the contrary, people having internal locus of control have confidence in themselves and their abilities. They take efforts and behave accordingly so as to change the situation. Such people show low anxiety and high self esteem. They also enjoy greater mental health.

It is also important to note that there is a continuum in between these two loci of control. The individual may not have the extreme or 100% inclination towards any end. Rather most of the people lie somewhere in between. Still, one of the patterns remains dominant.

Though it doesn't mean that to have internal locus of control is good or to have external locus of control is bad, but research in this area gives the following findings.

- **Locus of control and pro-social behavior:** Research suggests that there may a positive correlation between locus of control and altruism, as well as with self esteem. Thus those who are good in pro-social behavior are found to have high self esteem and hence internal locus of control.
- **Locus of control and behavioral differences:** People high in internal locus of control are less likely to have emotional problems. They understand the problems and cope with stress better. People with high external locus of control were found to be indecisive in new situations. External locus of control believers experience higher levels of work related stress and burnout.
- **Locus of control and health:** People high in internal locus of control have low stress, depression and less likely to develop loneliness.
- **Locus of control and gender:** Though some of the researchers suggest that men tend to have higher internal locus of control than women: but in many cases, there was no significant difference found in both genders on this variable. External locus of control appeared to increase in women soon after divorce, followed by a return to an internal locus of control. Similarly, women who were physically abused were high on external locus of control score.
- **Locus of control and culture:** Locus of control was found to be culture specific. Studies conducted showed that in general Asians have more inclination towards external locus of control than Americans. American culture promotes self reliance and individualism,

while Asian culture emphasizes community reliance and interdependence. But it was also found that more contact of Asians with Americans may bring change in locus of control from external to internal.

- **Locus of control and childhood:** Locus of control is shaped by childhood experiences. The children who were raised independently and who were educated to take responsibilities of consequences tend to develop internal locus of control. Children possessed high internal locus of control whose parents were found to be highly supportive, offering positive reinforcement, praising children for achievements and are consistent in discipline. It was also seen that cognitive training can bring shift in locus of control.

A factor that affects both internal and external locus of control is the stability of the underlying factor.

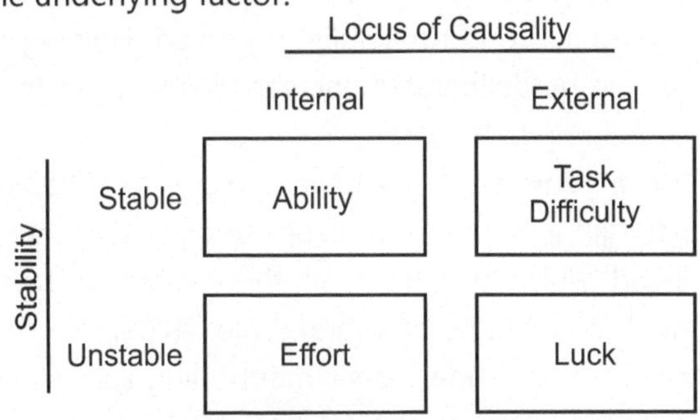

Fig. 3.7: Four common attributed causes

This table shown in Fig. 3.7 tells that the stability of fundamental factor affects both internal as well as external locus of control. A person with stable internal locus of control may assume failure due to lack of their ability, and person with unstable external locus of control justifies might say because they were unlucky.

3.3.2 Increasing Our Helping Nature

As you have read the previous sections, you have noticed that there are various shades in helping others. Whatever may be the form, the major objective is to make the world a better place. It is also one of the keys to happiness, as helping gives you satisfaction. Winston Churchill has nicely put "we make a living by what we get, but we make a life by what we give". Plenty of research shows that helping and giving can make you feel connected, grow in new ways and even live longer. As human beings are social in nature, we need relations for our psychological health. Connecting with others fulfills our need of being mentally fit. You may get connected by helping others, and by helping you creates new relations as well. Other that benefiting the other, you also get benefited by helping by many ways. Helping makes you feel grateful, builds your reputation, expands your identity, increases your self-esteem and keeps you away from stress. As giving makes us happy and happiness motivates us give more, an ever-ending cycle can be set.

As mentioned, pro-social behavior is subjective. Not everyone does it. Its true that everyone's character traits change little, so very less one can do about it. But the concept of neuroplasticity shows that any form training can reconfigure the brain, on both functional as well as on structural levels. When the individual is exposed to new situations consistently, then the ability to make changes in neurons and to attribute a new function to brain is made possible.

Thus, altruism may be purposefully improved. Helping nature which enriches our life can be deliberately increased. There are few ways which will increase our helping behavior.

- **Maintaining a journal:** While developing a new habit, it is always good to maintain a journal or a record book. A dedicated journal can be maintained which will have all the events or helps you have offered help. It may not be on grand scale. As help is not small or big, what matters is the attitude. Hence mentioning each small or big help must be recorded. Records also tell you whether you are helping the right person or not. The listing may contain sharing your tiffin, picking up grocery bags, calming a crying child, explaining a difficult math to a friend, clarifying an address to a tourist, holding the elevators for a person, etc. Such records act like reinforcement and help our behavior to occur again.
- **Being intentional:** Think that everyone on this planet is for purpose. Ask yourself about your meaning or intention of life. As each of us has got only one life, live on purpose. Try to make use of own life by making someone's life.
- **Be empathetic:** This is the most effective way of increasing helping behavior. When you will be able to understand the phenomenal world of others, you will be better able to understand his or her needs. Once you become empathetic, it will become easier to become more helpful. Empathy involves both affective and cognitive

components. It helps not only to feel the pain, but to understand the pain. Individuals with high empathy are motivated to help others more than individuals with low empathy. It encompasses three components. First, 'imagine other' – what other must be feeing perspective. Second, 'imagine self'-how I would feel if in that situation type perspective. Third perspective is 'fantasy feeling' for fictional character - in a book, movie, or television serial, thinking of what the characters must be going through perspective.

- **Build interpersonal relations:** If you are able to build trust and openness, then you will be able to become better helping person. People may not hesitate while asking for help to you if you remain trustworthy and open. To build good interpersonal relations, along with many other skills, one of the important skills is active listening skills, which you must cultivate.

  Offering a listening ear is itself a help you are offering! It also strengthens relationships and trust and people feel better and understood.
- **Give time:** In today's world, people are going through lot of emotional turmoil. Most of the people are becoming materialistic. If you can extend your help by sharing your time with the one who needs help, then that will be of greater value than any money-oriented help. Spending time is one of the precious services which reflects your love and care for them. It also shows that you respect them.
- **Have a positive approach:** Having a positive attitude and staying approachable helps others greatly. Helping doesn't always mean doing something in kind or material. Being optimist and supportive can also be a big help to many.
- **Be a volunteer:** Volunteering various social camps helps to enhance helping attitude. It also helps in increasing empathy. Participating in blood donation camps, helping flood victims, etc. may be the examples of offering help.

Fig. 3.8: Donating blood is thinking of others

3.4 Aggression

If you surf for popular games available online or on mobile, you will find almost all games are full of action and violence. Though virtually, people derive a lot of fun in shooting and killing others. The advertisements, slogans of those are full of blood, rifles or violence. Why people like violence? Why are people harboring extreme anger for others? Why they use abusive language, and behavior has become frequent? What type of hostile behavior people want to convey? Why people want to harm or damage others?

Aggression is one of the major emotions we have. It is one of the primitive emotions in human beings. Before civilizations, aggression was a need for defense, but still today the modern world also is full of aggression.

Every news channel and news paper is full of events like terrorism, bullying, crimes, religious riots, rapes, robbery, murders, suicides, arson, etc. Aggression is seen at home. Women and children are at risks even at homes. Aggression is observed in schools. Punishments, bullying are the examples of it. Even workplaces are at threat. Expressing resentment, obstructing the targets, physical assaults, racial comments, gender bias, sexual harassments, etc. are the examples of workplace aggression.

Such incidents not only disturb the societal harmony, but also leave inevitable consequences on generations. Thus studying aggression is a prime responsibility of social psychologists. What is aggression, how the nature of it is changing with modernization, what factors are responsible to generate that, how it can be controlled, etc. must be studied in depth.

3.4.1 Meaning of Aggression

In psychology, the term aggression is a behavior which is reflected as a reaction to frustration. An individual may get angry for a very small reason like someone cutting you in a queue or it can be a very strong reason like sexual abuse. It can be seen in the form of childish tantrums to suicidal acts. It can be a simple irritation caused by loud music around or it may be rage which can be seen when rights of an individual are violated.

In reaction, one may yell at or hit the other person, or one may even kill the other person. Smashing the fist on the table and killing the enemy in war is also an aggression. It can be seen clearly that aggression has number of shades, hence difficult to define unanimously.

Definitions: Social psychologists define aggression as follows-

- It is a behavior which is intended to harm another individual who does not wish to be harmed. **- Baron and Richerdson, 1994.**
- It is a harmful behavior which violates social conventions and which may include deliberate intent to harm or injure other person or property. **- Bandura, 1973.**
- The behavior aimed at harming others physically or psychologically. **– APA Dictionary.**

Aggression can be seen throughout the animal kingdom, involving resource competition and protection, which was one of the needs of survival. Considering these aspects aggression seems to carry negative as well as positive connotations.

3.4.2 Nature of Aggression

When we look around, we find there are people carrying hostile attitude to some extent for others. Anger is an emotion which is manifested as aggressive behavior. Remember the last time you lost your temper. How do you feel, if you come to your college for an extra lecture and then you come to know that the lecture has been cancelled? You obviously got annoyed, right? How did you react at such incidence?

When there is hindrance in achieving some predetermined goal, the individual gets frustrated. This frustration is the reason behind anger which is exhibited or expressed via some aggressive behavior. This expression may take any form such as physical, verbal, or emotional.

Fig. 3.9: Verbal aggression

Physical aggression involves harming someone physically e.g. hitting, kicking, stabbing, etc. Other non-physical expression of anger involves verbal, or emotional. It does not engage physical harm, but forms of yelling, shouting, screaming, etc. can be used to pressurize others. Emotional aggression may include not talking to other, inhibiting from doing something, keeping someone imprisoned, or starving someone, etc.

Other ways of nonverbal aggression also occur in the form of gossiping about specific person, spreading rumors, turning people against each other, blackmailing, excluding someone from the group, passing racial comments, texting sexual or offensive messages, flirting with another person to make someone jealous, etc. so as to harm the person mentally. The negative outcomes of physical aggression are quite obvious and sometimes the consequences are irrepairable. For example, if in the full of anger a person throws any valuable thing, it may get damaged permanently. An outraged person throws acid on any friend; her face will get injured forever. Let's understand the anger in detail.

Determinants of Aggression:

The reasons behind getting angry could be social, personal, and situational. People can be systematically provoked with the help of aggressive films or direct persuasion. An experiment on social learning by Bandura named 'Bobo Doll' experiment, or experiment on obedience by Milgram are well known on this account. These experiments showed that children can learn aggressive behavior by observational learning, and people can harm other persons when they are obeying some authority person. Mob lynching or stone pelting kind of activities are the examples of the fact that people can get easily influenced by societal pressure and flow with the aggression of crowd. Personal factors like type of personality, narcissism, ego, gender difference, etc are responsible for aggression. Influence of alcohol increases the aggression as well.

1. Expression of Anger:

One of the popular quotes by Aristotle can make you think about your reaction while expressing anger. He said, "Anybody can become angry - that is easy, but to be angry with the right person and to the right degree and at the right time and for the right purpose, and in the right way - that is not within everybody's power and is not easy."

Now, remember the way you expressed your anger, and ask few questions to yourself, whether it was for the right person, for the right reason, at the right time, and in the right way. Most of the times answers for some of these questions are negative. For example, in the college if the teacher scolds you, then you get irritated on your friend or on your mother. Here the person is not the right person on whom you are venting your anger out.

Expressing anger can be seen since childhood. Throwing tantrums during early childhood is considered as a part of normal developmental process because for them there is no other way to communicate their feelings. As verbal skills develop, children could communicate peacefully. Hence as we grow, expression of anger and motive behind anger get changed. Expression of anger may also take different forms. Sometimes the expression of anger can be intended or sometimes it may be a spontaneous reaction. Anger can be actively expressed which can be obvious observable behavior or it may take a form of passive aggression. From a relational perspective, passive aggressive behavior can be most difficult communication style to deal with because the other person doesn't understand what he is dealing with. Passive aggression may be inferred from behaviors like resenting the demands of others, saying 'no' to a request, delivering negative feedback, making complaints, procrastinating, making intentional mistakes, lack of appreciation, holding hostile attitude but presenting a warm and pleasant attitude, disguising criticism with compliments, etc.

Fig, 3.10: Withdrawal is passive aggression

2. **Types of Aggression:**

Aggression can be classified in following two types:

(a) Emotional or Impulsive Aggression: Impulsive aggression is characterized by strong emotions. This form is not planned and often comes into account during overwhelming state of mind. It triggers the acute threat response system which involves amygdale, and hypothalamus. It occurs with only a small amount of intent and determined by spontaneous reaction. Though the intent is small, but the outcome may be large enough. For example, if in a sport like wrestling, the opponent may tackle impulsively and cause serious harm. A short-tempered person may throw his mobile phone or television remote during any verbal fight.

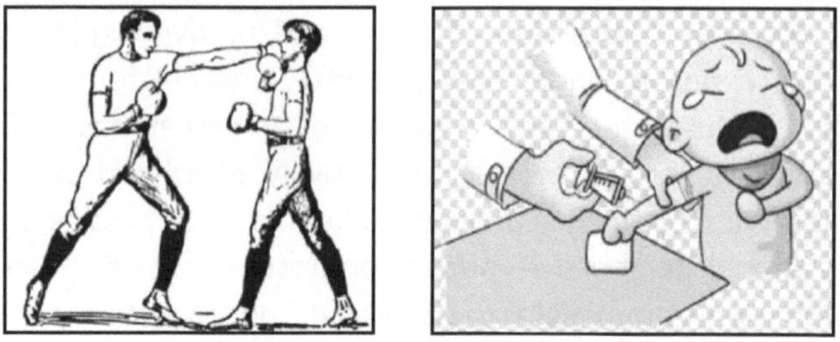

Fig. 3.11: Is this harming aggression?

(b) Cognitive or Instrumental Aggression: On the other side instrumental aggression is manifested by purpose of harm. It is more cognitive and may be cold and calculating. It involves planned aggressive behavior and intended to achieve larger goal- attention, monetary gain or political power etc. It may be seen as arson, bullying, robbery, murder, cyber bullying, etc.

Aggression takes into shape to express resentment, to claim dominance, to frighten, to express passion, to compete with others as we have to achieve goal, and in reaction to fear or pain. Examples of instrumental aggression can be given as a suicide bomber killing himself and many other people in crowd, spreading offensive photos of friend who betrayed, and like.

Thus it can be seen that aggression is one of the most complex behaviors seen in all living beings. In following section let us study what makes an individual angry.

3.4.3 Causes of Aggression

Do you remember last time when you lost your temper? What was the triggering incidence which made you annoyed? How do we learn to get angry? Whether it was in our genes? Or it was a learned activity? To what extent the human aggression is a matter of 'nature' or 'nurture'?

Aggression, like all other behaviors, involves biological factor, like genetic, hormonal, brain chemistry, etc. However, biological factor alone do not determine the development of aggressive behavior, but social, situational, and personal aspects also have great impact on aggression. Thus, it can be seen as aggression has multidimensional nature; causes of it are also varied. To find the answer and causes behind the question, why do human beings get angry with others, social psychologists and intellectuals have proposed various theories.

Following theories and approaches explain the nature of aggression:

1. Instinct theory:

This is one of the oldest and may be best possible explanation of human aggression. It argues that people are programmed to react aggressively. Before civilization, aggression was the basic reactions for protection of self and offspring. It was also used to fight with competition for getting resources. Aggressive behavior in animals, for example, threat, attack, and defense is commonly related to competition over resources, competition over mating opportunities, or fights for survival. It means that violence is inbuilt predisposition to oppose and get angry against others.

Konrad Lorenz, the famous zoologist said that aggression and fighting instinct in beast and man which is directed against members of same species is an inherited instinct. According to him, animals, particularly males are biologically programmed to fight over resources. Hence, aggression was part of natural selection. He said that this instinct has been developed during evolution as it helped to ensure that only the strongest and most vigorous individuals would pass their genes on to the next generation.

Aggression, the effects of which are frequently equated with those of the death wish, is an instinct like any other and in natural conditions it helps just as much as any other to ensure the survival of the individual and the species. As males who are skilled in such behavior may be successful in securing mates and transferring their gene to offspring, this may have developed the genetically influenced tendency for males to aggress against another male. On contrast, males would not become aggressive against females, as females may view males who fight as dangerous to themselves and potential future children, and hence may reject these males as potential mates. As a result, males have weaker tendency to aggress against females than against other males.

Sigmund Freud was also one of the proponents of this theory. He said that as people have a life instinct, they also have death instinct. He called death instinct as 'thanatos'. As per him, aggression is the overt behavior of strong death instinct. Death instinct is aimed to self destruction, but soon it gets diverted outwardly towards others.

2. Biological Approach:

Neuroscientists work to identify brain regions, genes, and neurotransmitters involved in aggression and violence. They have found that brain chemical serotonin, amygdale are also involved in aggression. The high presence of hormone testosterone has also been linked to increase acts of aggression.

3. Drive Theory Approach or Frustration - Aggression Hypothesis:

Miller and Dollard put their 'Frustration Aggression Hypothesis' where they say that frustration is the condition which exists when a goal response suffers interference. It states that aggression is always a consequence of frustration. Frustrating events are those which block the individual's goal orientated behavior. When an event or situation disturbs or upsets anyone, it is considered frustrating. But obviously a situation which is frustrating to one may not frustrate to other.

Here parental training, socio-economic status, and early childhood exposure for frustration tolerance play also role.

4. Social Learning Theory:

One day, a mother who heard abusive language from her 5 years son went to school to complain. But school denied as it was a remote chance for the child to learn that behavior from school. Ultimately, she realized that her son hears it from his father on the way to school when he drops him.

Social learning theory is a concept which explains aggression through direct observation. Albert Bandura conducted a series of experiments on children. His ground breaking study on aggression demonstrated that children are able to learn through the observation of adult behavior. He proposed the theory of social leaning. His experiments also found that males are somewhat more prone to imitate physical aggression - a highly masculine type behavior than females. While there was no difference in the imitation of verbal aggression which is less gender specific.

Social learning theory relies on the role of modeling, identification, and human interaction.

Learning through observation also depends upon many factors. If the model is not liked, or respected by the person, then his behavior may not be imitated. Children learn from parents as they like and respect parents.

As they have faith in parental behavior, they believe that parental behavior may not be wrong and hence there is no harm in following that behavior.

For example, if they observe the mother using harsh language with their maid, they will learn to show same reaction. This may be the reason that likes and dislikes of children are quite similar with mother. Likewise, a boy learns to be dressed like father or brother. If in case he wants to be dressed like a girl, then he learns from societal ridicule and understands that it is not liked by others. But after certain age with greater exposure to world, children start observing other people and learn via many resources.

Fig. 3.12: From where these children have learnt this behavior?

These theories tried to put scientific reasons for aggression. There are also other factors which seem to be responsible for aggression. They are as follows –

(i) Child abuse: Studies show that those who themselves had unhappy childhood, or whose emotional and psychological needs were not fulfilled, are more aggressive. They may also behave with their children aggressively. But those who were emotionally fit and had happy childhood, were also aggressive with children. Hence unsatisfied childhood of parents was not the only reason for aggressive behavior. Lonely parents, crowded homes, low socioeconomic status, illiteracy, being surrounded by criminal tendencies, malnutrition, child labor, etc. are responsible for child abuse.

(ii) Bullying and cyber bullying: Bullying is repeated assaults by one or more persons against a target person who is weaker or powerless. Research shows that the effect on bullying is not restricted to the victims, but also to bullies. This is one of very frequently seen behavior by children in schools and colleges. Bullying might make fun of others for many things like appearance, race, religion, sexual identity, etc. Bullying can come in various types as physical bullying, sexual assault, taunting, teasing, gossiping, excluding from group, threatening, etc.

Cyber bullying is now becoming more popular as the identity of the bully may be disguised. In this the bullies use internet and social media. Sending vulgar messages, offensive pictures, forcing someone to send their nude pictures, posting insulting comments on social media, asking for online transaction against some demand, blackmailing for posting someone's embarrassing content, etc. come under cyber bullying.

Nowadays anti-ragging squads are made easily accessible so that this type of notorious activity may be reduced. Cyber cells or safety apps are also made available in various schools and colleges.

But in any of the cases the victim must talk to a trusted adult and also must learn to deal with difficult people with confidence.

(iii) Social Media: In earlier days, dinner was the family time, where all family members used to have their meal at night with chatting with each other. It was one of the major activities for emotional bonding. All family members used to have sense of safety and warmth. But these days almost all family members spend their time more with virtual media than with people in person. Irrespective of ages, all members watch movies, web series, and television daily soaps. The content of such media is full of immorality, violence, frauds, fornications, etc. As elders of the family enjoy those, children also start believing those. It is becoming most influential factor in aggressive behavior in children.

(iv) Pornography and Sexual Torture: Most of the studies in this domain have concluded that these two factors are highly positively correlated. The criminals agreed that they were aroused after seeing such provoking porn films.

Easy access of such content via internet and literature has led into many distressing inferences like people do not feel miserable about rape victim, the acceptance regarding extra-marital relations is increased, people were ready to be aggressive themselves without feeling guilty, etc. Availability of weapons in the form of toys, uncensored media, attractive models or favorite actors displaying violent behavior, popular action heroes, mobile games portraying aggression, deteriorating values and morals in entertainment media etc. are having great impact on young and vulnerable minds. Unknowingly, children and adults as well are getting conditioned to violence and are losing their sensitivity as well as empathy.

Thus to summarize, it may be said that many chemicals have like testosterone, serotonin, societal and personal aspects like norms, values, self control, and culture of respect, use of alcohol etc. play major role in aggressive behaviors. Age and gender are important factors which may not be ignored.

Following section tells us how to reduce and prevent anger and aggressive behavior.

3.5 Applications: Prevention and Reducing Aggression

From the above discussion on aggression it may be noticed that it is one of the most complex behaviors of human beings. It has many aspects such as personal, social, situational, and cultural. Also, it has variety of shades in its intensity. It is the interaction of external events, cognition, and personal characteristics. Thus, if the triggering causes and the sources of aggressiveness are handled appropriately, one can lessen the aggression. Anger can be reduced and prevented as well, i.e. anger management is possible.

Nowadays the nature of aggression is becoming disastrous. Though it is difficult to reduce and stop aggression, it can be channelized so that it may be expressed in better way. The goal of anger management is to reduce both emotional and physiological arousal. As one cannot get rid of or avoid the events or people around, the only thing one may change is the oneself.

Few people are really hot headed than others, and get angry quickly and that too with greater intensity. Similarly, few people come from that family background, which is disruptive, chaotic and not skilled at emotional communication.

Though anger is a completely normal, and mostly a healthy emotion, but if it gets out of control and turn destructive, it may lead to problems. These may be at workplace, in relations, and quality of life in general. Here are some strategies to understand and control anger.

3.5.1 Anger Reduction and Punishment

As positive reinforcement or negative reinforcement can be used to enhance good behavior, punishment may be used to reduce bad or unwanted behavior. Punishment refers to the use of punisher to suppress or stop a response from occurring in the future. Use of punishment is seen all over the world as being effective. Whether punishments are useful or not is difficult to answer as there are both positive and negative consequences of punishment. For example, there was news that a teacher punished a student as he was getting notorious in school so as to reduce that behavior. But because of being insulted, that student stabbed that teacher. At the same time, it was also seen that if a class was penalized for not attending the classes, their absenteeism was reduced. Thus, punishment can be seen effective and ineffective as well.

Putting fines on breaking traffic rules, jail times for antisocial activities, asking a child for time out in the class or at home for misbehavior, giving a judgment of death sentence for murder, etc. are various examples of punishments.

While punishing, to make it maximally effective following things are to be considered. In other words, effectiveness of punishment depends upon a number of factors.

- **Use of Intense Punishment:** The more intense the punishment, the more effective it often is. Mild punishments tend to suppress behavior only temporarily. But at the same time, intense punishment carries the risk that a strong emotional response may be developed. For example, for a murder or a rape, intense punishments may prove useful; as it not only suppresses the behavior of the criminal, but also generates fear in others' mind which may help in reducing similar acts further. But while disciplining children, mild punishment to guide behavior may be most effective in long run. Still, too severe and too weak punishments both are ineffective.

  Punishment may be given in the form of physical or financial way.

- **Consistency in Punishment:** The more consistently punishment is administered, even if it is mild, the more effective it will be, if it is effective at all. Consistent punishments are more effective than inconsistent punishments. For example, if your mother asks you to clean plates if you don't finish your meals, but another day she says nothing. Then you will not understand what acceptable behavior is. Again in that the effectiveness of earlier punishment lessens.

- **Proximity of Behavior and Punishment:** The closer the punishment is in time and place to the behavior being punished, the more effective it will be. For example, a child is scolded by his parents after they return home from office for his misconduct in his school. Here the behavior and the punishment are not placed near each other. So the anticipated effect may not be seen. For a punishment to be most effective, it should be contingent upon the same behavior.
- **Frequent Punishment**: If people get adapted to punishment, this may weaken its effectiveness. For example, if the father shouts every here and then, then the child may get adapted and will not feel the severity.
- **Right Amount:** The punishment and the behavior must be related in amount. For example, for a small or trivial misbehavior, the punishments also must be relatively small. For example, our justice and law system do not punish lifetime imprisonment for pickpocketing.
- **Punishment and Explanation:** The punishment should probably be accompanied by simple and valid justification. It helps to understand precisely which behavior is unaccepted.

3.5.2 Catharsis

Catharsis hypothesis is the view which says that by providing an angry person an opportunity to express their aggressive impulse in relatively safe ways will reduce their tendencies to engage in more harmful form of aggression. Thus if an individual gives vent to his anger in relatively less harmful way, the anger subsides and the tendency to get engaged in destructive acts lessens. But this popular belief was contradicted by research findings, as the vigorous activities may produce temporary reduction in arousal but feeling of anger may quickly return when the triggering situation or person reappears.

3.5.3 Cognitive Intervention

- **Changing the way of thinking:** Cognitive restricting means changing thinking patterns. It has been seen that usually angry people tend to curse, swear, or speak abusive. These behaviors reflect their inner thoughts. Angry people may think exaggerated and act overly dramatic.

Usually people want things, but the one who is angry, makes demands. And when the demand is not met, he or she becomes angry. As a part of restructuring, an angry person must be aware of his demanding nature. He should learn to understand the difference between demands and expectations. He may say, "I would like to have it" rather, "I must get it".

Similarly, before talking or reacting, the person should develop the habit of thinking the probable consequences of his anger and aggressive behavior.

Whenever possible the person also may try to use humor.

- **Apologies:** You must have many people find it difficult to say sorry and apologize. Apologies are admitting the wrong doings. For that people first accept that they also can be wrong, or make mistakes. Similarly, people must also get the broad mindedness which allows forgiving others.
- **Understand the provoking events and person:** For this one should maintain a log book which may include the incidences which make one angry. Which type of situation or what type of people, one does not get along well. If one can formulate these factors, then he may be mentally prepared to face them, and also if possible, avoid them.
- **Changing the environment:** If you find you are stuck in the aggressive moment or unavoidable situation which makes you angry, then changing the environment can be a good strategy. For example, when angry, go walking, jogging, gardening etc. Else listen to smoothening music, watch comedy movie, using the energy onto sport, etc.

Fig. 3.13: Constructive way of anger management

- **Relaxation and meditation:** Simple relaxation techniques like deep breathing, using imagery, keeping calm can help you to come down the angry feelings.

  Practices like meditation, breathing techniques also help in long run.
- **Communicate:** This technique is more helpful for everyone and especially for those who are passive aggressive. Passive aggressive behavior unnecessarily consumes time and resources, instead saying what one wants to convey, and resolve the issue can be a better way of handling anger. It allows to move on to more productive tasks. Keeping grudges in mind, accumulating the negativity results in diverting anger inwards. The outcome of it may lead to ill health.

✧ Exercise ✧

Q. 1 : *Answer the following questions in brief :*

(1) What is interpersonal attraction? Give definition.

(2) Explain relation between locus of control and influence of culture.

(3) Give the impact of punishment on aggression.

(4) Explain interpersonal relations beyond family.

Q. 2 : *Answer the following questions in detail :*

(1) Explain in detail the use of cognitive intervention to reduce aggression.

(2) Explain in detail ways to increase pro-social behavior.

(3) Explain the theories of interpersonal attraction.

(4) Elaborate Sternberg's triangular theory of love.

Q. 3 : *Write short notes :*

(1) Pro-social behavior.

(2) Causes of aggression.

(3) External determinants of interpersonal attraction.

(4) Catharsis – Way to reduce aggression.

✧ Questions from Previous University Exams ✧

(1) *Describe the triangular theory of love.* **(April 2016)**

(2) *Explain in brief the forms of aggression.* **(April 2016)**

(3) *What is pro social behavior?* **(April 2017)**

(4) *Which are the internal and external factors influencing pro social behavior?* **(April 2016)**

(5) *Write short notes on internal determinants of attraction.* **(April 2017)**

(6) *What is attraction?* **(October 2017)**

(7) *What are levels of aggression?* **(October 2017)**

(8) *Explain causes of aggression.* **(October 2017)**

☆☆☆

UNIT – 4

GROUP DYNAMICS

SYNOPSIS

4.1 Groups

- 4.1.1 Definition and Types of Groups
- 4.1.2 Characteristics of Groups
- 4.1.3 When We Join and When We Leave
- 4.1.4 Benefits of Joining Groups

4.2 Cooperation and Conflict

- 4.2.1 Cooperation
- 4.2.2 Conflict

4.3 Social Influence

- 4.3.1 Social Influence – Definitions
- 4.3.2 Conformity
- 4.3.3 Factors Affecting Conformity
- 4.3.4 Using Conformity for Healthy Behavior
- 4.3.5 Obedience and Authority
- 4.3.6 Compliance

4.4 Group Decision Making

- 4.4.1 Formation of Group
- 4.4.2 Definition of Group Decision Making
- 4.4.3 Stages and Steps in Group Decision Process
- 4.4.4 Nature of Group Decision
- 4.4.5 Techniques of Group Decision

4.5 Application : Team Building

- 4.5.1 Building a Dream Team
- 4.5.2 Benefits of Team building

✧ Exercise

4.1 Groups

Do you have students in your college who are from various parts of country? Then probably you must have observed that they form a group and stay together. If you are staying in a foreign country, and one day on road you hear someone talking in your language, perhaps you feel happy because in that unfamiliar crowd, you find someone from your nation i.e. from your group of people. Every person wants to be with others. Basically human being likes to be with a group.

To stay in a group is one of the instincts we possess. Hence, when a newborn; who is unaware of surrounding becomes calm if it finds himself with its caretaker. To stay with group was one of the major decisions made by human beings.

Our lives are highly influenced by nature of the group and the membership we have. It remained beneficial for human being to form and stay on group. Social psychologists try to find the answers to questions like what are the characteristics of group, why human beings want to stay in groups, why and when they either join or leave any group.

Allport, Bandura, Festinger, Tajfel, Turner, Milgram, Zimbardo, etc. are few highly influential social psychologists who performed innovative experiments which throw light on person's behavior in social structure.

Introduction:

When people assemble to watch any movie in a theater, are they a group? When you play a football match opposite another class, are you a group? What makes a group?

Though people have gathered at a theatre to watch movie, but they are not interdependent on each other and also they have not been assigned defined roles, status and expectations from each other. Hence they do not form a group in true sense. But if we consider these factors as criteria for a group, then your family, class or your sports team will be the examples of groups.

The study of group dynamics in sociology and psychology can find its roots long back in late nineties. Wilhelm Wundt (1832-1920) showed interest in psychology of communities. He said that possessed phenomenon like language, customs, and religion could not be described through the study of the individual. Kurt Lewin coined the term group dynamics. He established a research centre at MIT, Cambridge in 1945, which was the first institute to study of group dynamics.

Group dynamics refers to a system of behaviors and psychological processes within groups and between groups. People gather together and become a part of collection to form a group. But it is not easy to define what makes a group of people to form a social group. For example, if you are standing in queue to buy a ticket, then those gathering of people cannot be considered as a group because they are not meaningfully related to each other. A gathering of people watching a sport on the ground also may not be considered as a group, because they just happened to be at same place at the same time. But they are not connected as a social group. They are only sharing a common interest. These various types of gatherings of people can be differentiated as a crowd, team or audience.

Crowd is also collection of people. But they may be present at that particular place by chance. They are neither structured nor have feeling of belongingness. Their behavior may be irrational and have no interdependence. For example, people at shopping at mall.

Audience, on the other side is a group as well, but it is the collection of individuals who have gathered for special purpose such as to watch a movie.

But a team is a special kind of group. Usually the members of a team are gathered together as they possess a specific skill. They are committed to achieve a common goal.

A group is relatively permanent, while crowd and audience are short lived in nature. Another major distinction is that in a crowd there is emotional excitement that is absent in a group. The members of group behave in somewhat organized, constructive and civilized manner and show value based activities. While imitation and irresponsibility etc. is observed in crowd than in a group.

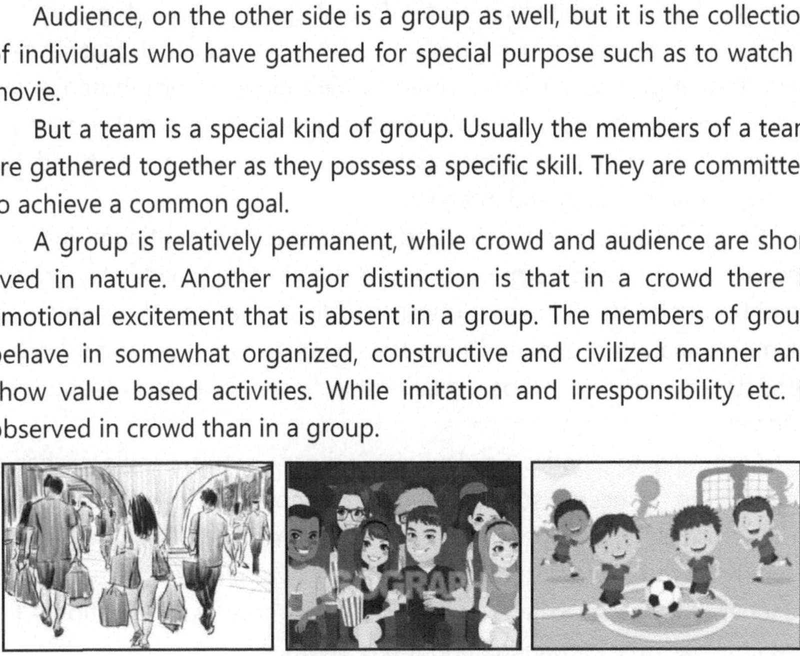

Fig. 4.1: Crowd, Audience and Team

4.1.1 Definitions and Types of Groups

Various psychologists, sociologists have defined 'group' from different perspectives. Hence no uniformity is found in all those. Few of the definitions are as follows-

- "It is social unit consisting of number of individuals interacting with each other with respect to common motive and goals, accepted division of labor, established status of relationships, accepted norms and values with reference to matters relevant to group."

  - Muzafer Sherif (1969)

- "A group consists of two or more persons engaged in social interaction who have some stable structured relationship with one another, are interdependent, share common goals and perceive that they are in fact part of a group". **- Baron and Byrne (1988)**

Thus in general a group may be defined as an organized system of two or more individuals who are interacting with each other and are interdependent. It is an organized system of more individuals who are related to one another so that it performs some functions.

There are various types of groups depending upon the function; for example formal, semiformal and informal groups. Formal groups are typified by rules and order such as group in an industrial organization. Semi formal groups act less formally, where power is distributed across the group. Also it has more collaborative approach. Informal groups are friendship or interest groups. This type of group is less structured and usually based on liking and interests.

Groups also can be categorized by more or less continued intimate association. They can be primary group such as family; kids play groups, neighborhoods etc. Primary group is usually a small social group whose members share personal and long lasting relationship. Secondary group consists of members whose relationships are interpersonal and goal oriented.

According to Charles Cooley, in a primary group people exchange love, caring, concern, support, encouragement, etc.; while secondary groups usually share special interest, for example, professional groups. Their relationships are temporary. They are termed as secondary, as generally they develop later in life. They also have weak emotional ties and little personal knowledge about one another.

Fig. 4.2: Primary and secondary groups

4.1.2 Characteristics of Groups

Groups have the following significant characteristics:

- Collection of two or more people in social interaction forms the smallest group. Group helps in distinguishing one group from the other and gives the group its unique identity.
- A group can be identified by the specific behavior patterns of the individuals within the group.
- Every member of a group shares common goals or interests and also has a common fate or future. Groups function either working towards a given goal, or away from certain threats.
- The group members are mutually related to one another. It is regarded as group's important and distinctive feature. Because aggregate of individuals cannot constitute a group unless reciprocal awareness exists among them.
- All the members of a group are interdependent on each other. It means behavior of any of the members may have consequences on others. For example, all the artists performing on stage are members of a group. While performing, if any of the actors from the cast forgets his dialogues, then it may affect on the performance of the group as a whole.
- All the members who interact are structured by a set of standard roles and norms of behavior of performance.
- Members who are trying to motivate and satisfy a need through joint involvement also influence each other.
- Interaction and interdependence of the group members either physically or virtually to achieve the group goal is one of the major features of a group.

- Groups have a collective identity. They are composed of people who recognize each other as a member of their group and can distinguish them from non-members.
- Each group requires having a sense of unity and "we"-feeling.
- Cohesiveness is one of the major features of groups. It is a strong and enduring bond among members. When the members have strong and enduring bonds, their morale is high and they possess a general sense of belonging. While in some groups, members are loosely joined and have lack of sense of community. Thus cohesiveness refers to both positive and negative forces that cause members to remain in a group. When members like each other, cohesiveness is high. If the interaction is effective and in agreement, then it leads to minimal conflicts. This is a major reason for bonding of the group. High level of cohesiveness is beneficial for running of the group.
- The existence of a group is due to the members in it. Also, the group gives the individual a different identity. Therefore, the magnitude of the individual's influence on the group and effect of group on the individual are complementary. Hence there is always an interaction going among an individual and the group.
- It is also important to see that the membership norms and standards of the group are not in breach. Maintaining a sense of belonging among the members of the group is a crucial aspect of the group's survival. Within the group, the members must be connected to each other with an integrated spirit, hence it is important for the head of the group to have check that there is minimal conflict among the members.

Thus in a nutshell it can be said that factors which are important in the functioning of a group are roles, sense of belonging, interdependence, norms, etc.

4.1.3 When We Join and When We Leave

As we take birth, we become a member of a family as a group without choice. But many times to become a part of group is a conscious decision of an individual.

While joining any group, if an individual likes some of the individuals in the group, then it becomes bond-based attachment and when he or she likes that specific group, then the group has identity-based attachment.

An individual may have either strong personal connection with other members or the interest in the group as a whole entity.

According to scientists as Dasgupta, Banerjee, and Abelson (1999), members need to be emotionally connected with others to form a group. Based on this criterion, two types of groups can be formed common-bond group and common-identity group. They are also can be called as shared relationship group and shared identity group. Both of the types of group formation generate strong commitments but in different ways.

Thus as, joining a group or formation of a group is based upon different motives, the two types of groups have different and well defined features in terms of group dynamics, patterns of interaction, subgroup structure, individual commitment, etc.

1. **Common-Bond group** may be said as the group which tends to have face-to-face interaction and in which the individual members are bonded to each other. For example, members in a family, group of a cricket team, group of your classmates, colleagues of an office, etc. As they interact personally, they are emotionally bonded to each other.
2. **Common-Identity Group** is that where face to face interaction is often absent, and the members are linked together via the category as a whole rather than each other. For example, all students of your college from some state, or all the residents from housing society having same mother tongue, etc. Though every member of such group do not know each other, but having some common link or connection, keeps them attached to that group.

People get membership of different groups depending on emotional, mental or other needs and goals which are required to be reached at that particular moment. When the need for attachment is higher, then people remember the common or shared bond group. For example, if you are in a major financial problem, then you may seek help from member of common bond group like your friend or some of the relatives. On the other hand, when the need for identity is more, then common identity group will be remembered. For example, a student who takes admission for higher education at a different state or a country; tries to get connected to a group of his own community.

This could have been the probable cause of formation of such organizations like *Maharashtra Mandal* in various countries.

Fig. 4.3: Need to form a group based on identity

Thus, it may be summarized that the individual becomes committed to a group i.e. when he decides to join or leave any group depends on two different ways:

- Through group members' personalization of specific features of the group e.g. norms, stereotypes, common interests, group history, etc.
- Through interpersonal attractions among individual group members.

An individual may join any group depending upon the need. Group members have certain common goals, but at the same time, they have their individual goals or interests. At this stage there may be conflict in achieving common goal with fulfillment of individual goals. So when people find that the interests with which they joined any group are not fulfilled, then they may leave the group. According to one of the surveys by Pew Research Center's Internet and American Life Project (2010), an individual's reason for exiting from any group may vary from lack of group leadership to losing interest in the goals of the group. Following chart shows the major reasons for what compels someone to leave a group from the survey.

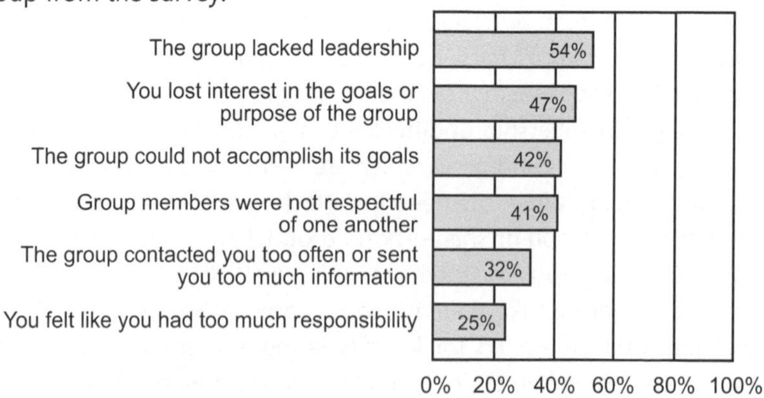

Source : Pew Research Center's Internet and American Life Project, November 23 - December 21, 2010 Social side of the Internet Survey. N for active members of groups = 1,833

Fig. 4.4: Few reasons to leave the social group

4.1.4 Benefits of Joining Groups

It is difficult for any individual to satisfy his mental, physical, social, or financial requirements on his own. Similarly, needs like food, clothing, shelter, cohabitation, safety, etc. are impossible to accomplish without help as well. McClelland's theory of need of achievement gives emphasis on the importance of interpersonal relations. If people feel socially isolated, then they may face mental health problems more than those who are connected well socially. A recent study published in Australian and New Zealand Journal of Psychiatry by Saeri, AK & et.al (2018) tells that increasing one's level of social connection can protect one's mental health.

Joining the group may prove beneficial to both, an individual and the group as well. For example, if a football player joins any sports group, then he gets benefits of coaching, backing of the team, availability of resources, etc. At the same time, the group also gets the advantage of the name and fame of that specific player.

Similarly, people also accomplish many things as a part of a group that they could not accomplish on their own. For instance, an individual is quite social and wants to work for humanity. In that case if he joins a group like Red Cross society or any NGO working for people, then in that case he gets proper guidance, funding, human resource, and opportunities to work.

Groups also make more productive decisions than an individual could make. When more people work and think together; important, challenging and sometimes risky decisions are made more than an individual may make.

Thus, being a member of any group is advantageous.

Every individual is a member of many groups at a time. For example, you can be a member of group like your classmates, relatives, people from your cast, race, ethnicity, etc. Along with these you can also be a member of some sports team or various other activity groups from your college.

Different groups satisfy different needs. People join groups because every individual has different needs. Mostly we automatically become a member of groups which are based on the cast, religion, race, nationality, etc. But decision to join any group which is based on interests and motives is made deliberately.

In today's modern era, one cannot survive solitary without the help of others. Togetherness is very significant. To live effectively it is necessary to remain associated with others.

In general, people join various groups for the following reasons:

1. **Security:** Since childhood, if an individual is alone, feels insecure. Being a part of group makes one feel safe. It gives comfort and protection. The fear of standing alone is greatly reduced when in group. In group, people are more resistant to threats. This is probably the strongest reason for group formation.
2. **Status:** An individual gets an identity when being affiliated to a group. It gives a feeling of pride. For example, if your college wins a trophy in certain sport, you feel proud of being a student of your college. Obviously it helps in boosting your esteem. Being a member of group helps an individual to enhance his self concept. (Tajfel and Turner, 1979). The membership of a group provides opportunities for recognition and honour that are not available outside the group. For example, if a person is working as a manager in one of the companies, then he will get respect and admiration till he is holding that post. As soon as he leaves from that post, he is treated as an ordinary person.

   Social groups across all species self organize into hierarchies of the positions. Under that hierarchy, members vary in their positions, power, skills, influence etc. For a group positions or ranks are the important features. Different roles or status are associated with them. Organizing the group in such hierarchical manner is the effective way to maximize group unity and productivity too. For example, for any organization to run smoothly, various posts like Chairman, Director, Secretary, etc. are generated.
3. **Affiliation:** One of the major reasons of joining a group is that people enjoy the company of like-minded people, especially when the group is formed on same interest grounds. People share their experiences to enrich their lives. They also provide knowledge and information which broadens their view. Many of the intellectual, mental and emotional needs can be satisfied by joining any group.
4. **Power:** Group membership offers power to an individual. As per the saying, "united we stand, divided we fall", being united makes you feel stronger. Also working together always is more enjoyable than working alone.

Fig. 4.5: Unity may help even to survival

5. **Goal Achievement:** For institutes to run, organizations to function, or a team to win more than one person is required. A pool of talents is necessary to complete any task. To achieve any tough goal, group members work in collaboration. For instance, imagine an individual climbing the Everest Mountain. Achieving this tough goal alone will be extremely difficult. Hence such activities are always accomplished as a group in the form of a team.

   Though there are large numbers of benefits of being a part of a group, few may have negative experience as a group member.

4.2 Cooperation and Conflict

People interact with each other in different contexts. This interaction is in the form of behavior. In most social situations the outcomes can be cooperation, competition or conflict. For example, if one day when you remain absent for some reason in a college, then you ask your friend what was taught that day, what the teacher asked to do, etc. If that friend tells you all the revelations, then you may also help him later, but if the friend refuses to help you, then you probably remember that and you would also refuse to help him later. In other words, you decide whether to cooperate or have conflict with him. Similarly, if you score highest marks in class in a subject, then other classmates will try to compete with you. Same way to bring vegetables, fruits, etc. while going home from the office as per mother's instructions; is also a cooperative behavior.

In general, it can be said that usually there are three types of behavior co-operation, competition and conflict.

Cooperation is when two or more people have common goal and they work together to accomplish. Competition is when two or more people strive against one another to gain possession of some goods or service. Conflict is a deliberate action when one individual attempts to thwart the will of another. These three are important aspects of management of individuals in a society.

In cooperation, people help each other, share knowledge and information, and work for same objective. In competition people try to prevent other person for being able to gain the limited resource or reward. But whenever there is disagreement in the motives or goals to achieve; conflict arises. During conflict, more importance is given to individual's goal.

In earlier chapter you have studied about pro-social behavior which has no intention of any benefit or gain. But it is normally seen that many people help other because of some intention of gain, mostly mutual gain. In this pattern of behavior, both parties achieve their motives in some or other way. This type of behavior is termed as cooperation. However, when the personal interests seem to be unachievable, then in that case instead of working together, people work against each other. This is called as conflict.

It was always observed and experienced that working in cooperation has been beneficial to those who are involved. Then why does conflict occur? Why can't we all get along? The answer to this question is in the meaning of cooperation itself. Cooperation is seen when people make every effort to achieve shared or common goal. But the goals like getting promoted for one post, trying to get engaged with a romantic partner, etc. conflict will be obviously unavoidable. Cooperative goal is one in which each individual can attain goal only if other member of the group also attains goal. On the contrary, competitive goals are laid down when one member can attain goal at the expense of others achieving it. It is interesting to note that competition between two persons leads to conflict or dissonance, while competition between two groups may increase cohesion and unity within group.

4.2.1 Cooperation

It is an integrated activity and considered to be opposite of competition. It literally means working together and involves two elements- common goal and organized efforts. Cooperation is evolutionarily useful for human being. Because of cooperation, human race has survived. Thus cooperation for human beings is both a psychological and social necessity. Social norms and social order could not be maintained without cooperation. Cooperation is possible because of factors like desire for individual benefit, wish to give and share, and desire to achieve higher, larger goal.

1. Factors Affecting Cooperation:

Factors like reciprocity, personal orientation and communications are major factors which decide whether the person will cooperate or compete.

(a) Reciprocity Principle: This is obvious tendency of human being. People usually follow the principle or rule of 'Tit-for-Tat', which is equivalent retaliation. It means we treat others as they have treated us. In choosing between cooperation and competition people seem to take up this rule. When people help us, we tend to help them; when people cooperate with us, we tend to be kind to them. While, if people are becoming obstacle in achieving our goal, we reciprocate in the same way.

(b) Personal Orientation: In your life you must have met with many experiences where you have seen people who help others irrespective of benefit. They are helping in nature. They usually avoid arguments and also may show selfless behavior. Whether on playground with friends, at home with family members or at workplace few people show cooperative nature. People who are self centered, aggressive or skeptical in nature; believe less in cooperation.

(c) Communication: Communication is exchange of ideas and information. Therefore if it occurs to develop understanding, know the goals of self and others, and come to a consensus, then that may lead in collaboration than competition or conflict. Effective communication may lead to cooperation.

This factor influences to a great extent whether to choose cooperation or to compete. The effectiveness of any content or message to be conveyed lies in the way it is conveyed.

2. Social Dilemmas:

In our daily life we experience many such incidences where we realize that cooperation would have been sorted the problem than competition. But at the time of decision making people face dilemma. After consequences they may realize that probably cooperation would have been a better choice. This fact was proved by many social psychologists through experiments on social dilemmas. Some of them are as follows:

(a) The Robber's Cave (Summer Camp Experiment): Mujafer Sherif, one of the famous social psychologist, conducted a series of experiments in 1966 on school boys from middle class background who did not know each other. All the boys were at a summer camp at Robber's Cave, Oklahoma, America. Unknown to boys, there were researchers in the camp who were observing the boys' behavior. This experiment which led to the formation of Realistic Conflict Theory is considered to be a classic study on intergroup cooperation and conflict. It demonstrated how groups strongly favor their own members (in-group bias), and how intergroup conflict can be resolved by groups working together for common goal. By these experiments Sherif proved that conflict and hostility arise when there is competition for limited resources.

In this experiment, boys were divided into two groups. They were unaware of the intention of experiment; rather they were assuming that they have been taken for a camp. The researchers were camp instructors.

The study was divided into four stages.

(i) **Friendship formation:** Boys spent initial time together, mixed freely and chose their friends.

(ii) **In-group formation:** The boys were then divided into two groups. The boys belonging to different groups lived separately. All the members from the group eventually developed their own norms and got united with increasing cohesiveness.

(iii) **Inter-group competition:** Both the groups were then brought together for various competitions like matches. This competition developed sense of rivalry and hostility against each other. At the same time in-group faithfulness increased.

(iv) **Inter-group cooperation:** Then to reduce this antagonist environment, researchers created a problem which affected both the groups. They wanted to see if the conflict that has built could be resolved by introducing a common goal where everyone will have to work with each other. For this, both the groups were shifted to new location where the water supply of both groups was disrupted. In this scenario, members of both groups helped each other to overcome this common problem. This increased the inter-group cooperation and reduced the inter-group conflict.

This experiment proved that hostility can be generated by group situations, and can be reduced by focusing on super-ordinate goals which are vital and favorable to both groups.

(b) Prisoner's Dilemma: This so called game is one of the most extensively studied and explored in social psychology. In this two individuals acting in their own self interests do not produce the optimal outcome. It is set up in such a way that both participants choose to protect themselves at the cost of other. Ultimately both of them find themselves in worse state than if they would have been cooperating with each other.

This game theory paradox was developed by mathematicians M. Flood and M. Dresher in 1950, while the modern interpretation of it was by A.W. Tucker.

To understand prisoner's dilemma imagine that the police arrested two suspects of a crime. Both suspects are kept separately so that they cannot communicate. The police officer offers the opportunity to each of them to either remain silent or blame another suspect. If both remain silent, both will serve only one year imprisonment. If both blame each other, they will serve three years in prison. If one of the suspects blames another and other remains silent, the one who remained silent would get five years of punishment and another suspect would be set free.

Suspect B / Suspect A	Remain silent	Blame
Remain silent	1 / 1	0 / 5
Blame	5 / 0	3 / 3

Fig. 4.6: Prisoner's Dilemma

Fig 4.6 explains that if both the suspects would have been remained silent, i.e. cooperated with each other, both of them would have been benefitted with minimal punishment. But as per setting, both suspects did not know the decision made by another suspect. Hence to protect self interest, each suspect blames another despite of worst payoff.

Thus, it can be shown with the help of this example from game theory that in a non-cooperative situation, even a more attractive approach can lead to poorer results.

There are many more famous experiments where social psychologists have studied many factors, such as cooperation, conflict, and competition by creating various incidents and conducting different field experiments.

4.2.2 Conflict

Daily routine experiences conflicts. It has become the part of social life. They are inseparable and significant part of human life on every level of interaction. There are various types of conflicts such as inter-personal, intra-group, inter-group, inter-organizational and international conflicts as well. Sadly it is a fact that for most of the conflicts humans have paid a big price. Let us know more about conflicts, its nature, causes.

1. Nature of Conflicts:

As mentioned, conflict is a conscious action. It is a purposeful intention to oppose. As per Sigmund Freud the innate instinct for aggression is the main cause of conflicts. A.W. Green (1956) defined it as "the deliberate attempt to oppose, resist or coerce the will of others". In conflict, there is intense feeling of 'we' and 'they'. There is also a belief by both members that the other will protect its own interest and hence obviously, their (other's) interest will not be protected. In conflict, there is not only disagreement between the groups or two members, but also a rivalry and tries to overpower each other. Hence, conflict experiences feeling like aggression, jealousy, hostility, etc.

Conflicts take place constantly and continuously. Because it is not possible for almost every human being to allow and accept disagreements over goals, motivations, aspirations, needs, etc. Though conflicts create disharmony, they are necessary for progress and innovations. Because if a person is restricted from something, then only he is expected to get it from some other way using new idea.

Conflicts helped to eliminate many malpractices like discrimination, inequality, exploitation, etc.

2. Causes of Group Conflicts:

Mentioned below are few causes for group conflicts.

- **Lack of effective communication:** It results in distrust, doubt, jealousy, and misunderstanding. These factors lead to the feeling of difference and ultimately end up in conflict.
- **Relative deprivation:** This is a very commonly seen reason amongst people. When people have the feeling that they are not getting what they deserve and on the contrary the one who is getting the same does not deserve. This comparison between groups or between the members of groups leads to conflict.
- **Feeling of superiority:** Conflicts occur when one believes to be better than other and wishes others to treat oneself respectfully.
- **Past experiences:** If there is some harm which was done in past to a person, then that could be the reason of arising conflict.

3. Resolution Strategies of Group Conflict:

If the causes of conflicts are handled at sources, then conflicts can be resolved. Following are the few strategies for conflict resolution.

- **Super ordinate goal:** If two members or two groups are found to be in conflict, then introduction of super ordinate common goal may help in communication, cooperation and hence conflict resolution.
- **Increasing intergroup contacts:** Though conflicts are there, but if the intergroup contacts are intentionally increased on neutral grounds through team games and activities, conflicts may be lessened.
- **Negotiating:** Conflicts can be reduced by intervention of third party and negotiations so that reciprocal communication could take place.

4.3 Social Influence

While walking on roads, if you find that few people are looking up in sky, then do you also look up? Probably yes. While driving a car if you find someone wearing khaki color uniform asking you to show your vehicle documents, then instead of seeing the authority and authenticity of the person, you may do what they ask as we come under pressure of uniform and assume that the person has authority.

If you come across with an advertisement, "Hurry... offer ends today!", then perhaps you are tempted to purchase that particular thing. Such reactions to social stimuli are automatic and often unconscious.

When we experience such incidences, we must agree with the very famous quote, by an American writer and political commentator Walter Lippman, "When all think alike, then no one thinks very much". This is social influence. This thought by Lippman was also taken by Robert B. Cialdini, reputed emeritus professor and psychologist at University of Arizona who worked on social influence.

4.3.1 Social Influence - Definitions

Social influence forces us to change our thought, and behavior. Many students take admission to any course because of many other choose that stream. If many of your friends use mobile phone of some specific brand, then you too wish to have the same. Mostly people want to follow as they do not want to become odd man out. Social influence is defined as follows.

- "Social influence is the tendency to change one's behavior to match the behavior of others." - **Cialdini and Goldstein, 2004.**
- "Social influence as the efforts by one or more individuals to change the attitudes, beliefs, perceptions, or behaviors of one or more others." - **Cialdini, 1994.**
- When one person's actions lead to another person's actions, it is said to have a social impact." - **Paul Secord and Carl Backman, 1964.**

Thus it may be said that human behavior is influenced by society and societal norms. This influence forces us to change our actions to meet social demands. In the next section let us study three major types of social influence which are conformity, obedience to authority and compliance.

4.3.2 Conformity

Conformity refers to the act of changing one's behavior to match with others. It is the likeness or similarity of behavior. The one who tries to accept the same behavior is called as conformist. Usually people lack confidence in their knowledge, and they take help of others with the hope that they will be furnished with correct information. To accept the information is to confirm with them. In other words the person gets subjected to social influence.

- **Mujafer Sherif - Conformity and Group Norms**: Psychologist Mujafer Sherif demonstrated in his classic experiment on auto kinetic effect of conformity in 1935 (The auto kinetic effect is an illusion, where the small light in a dark room which does not actually move, but appears to be in moving). He took participants in a dark rook and told to stare a small, stationary pinpoint of light and to report how far it moved. In first phase of the experiment, he recorded the observations made by people individually. In second phase, a group of participants were placed in the dark room. He found that people, who estimated larger distance individually, came to an agreement with others with lesser distance. And who found lesser distance settled with larger distance. This showed that people change their opinion in presence of others' opinions. Therefore individuals will adjust their own behavior to accept and confirm the group norms.

- **Solomon Asch - Conformity and Group Pressure:** The most significant experiment on conformity was by Solomon Asch in 1951. In his research, he showed the participants printed standard line of a given length and they have to match the length of it to the comparison lines.

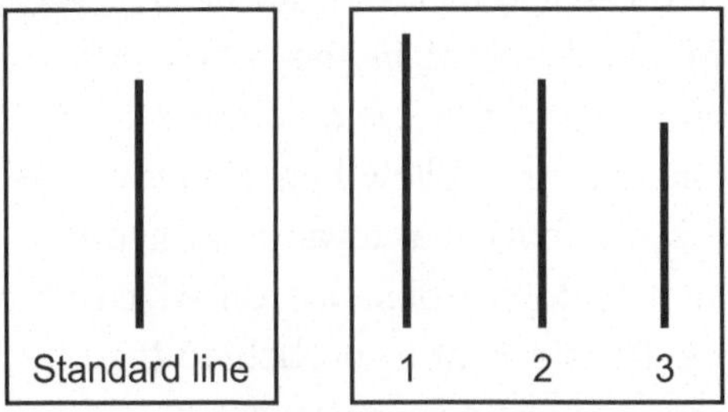

Fig. 4.7: Stimuli used by Asch

In a group setting, the participants were asked to report individually (but in presence of all) which of the lines was the same as that of the standard line. The participants were unaware of the fact that in the group of participants, the other group members were confederates who are the persons working for researcher. The confederates were instructed to deliberatively give wrong answers. Even when the correct answer was very clear, Asch found that participants would confirm the answer given by group and report obviously incorrect answer.

It shows that social influence, group pressure can lead the person to doubt their own knowledge when it is opposed by other group members.

The conclusions obtained from such path breaking experiments have been applied across many situations. For example, voters may turn out and give confirmatory behavior while electing any candidate in presence of other voters. For this reason open voting is not recommended.

Social pressure is seen everyday situation. We always follow to stand in any line at a ticket window ,just because other people do it. We also try to follow current trends in fashion or even while choosing educational stream.

Adopting habits may be good or bad is also a part of conformity. One of the most interesting examples of conformity is getting married. Marriage is the major confirmatory behavior. People marry because most of the people do that.

4.3.3 Factors Affecting Conformity

Why people follow the trend? Why people want to be in accordance with others? Why we want to go along with group? Let us understand which factors are responsible for conformity behavior.

- **Cohesiveness - Accepting influence from those we like:** After Balakot attack in February 2019, you must have noticed many men suddenly started keeping their moustache style which was like one of the Indian officers' involved in the attack. Many males who were influenced and impressed by wing commander Abhinandan, wanted to change their style and follow him. Cohesiveness is the degree of attraction felt by an individual towards someone or some group. To whom you want to follow depends on which of the two you find more attractive. People want to go behind the one who is successful and popular than the one who is unsuccessful.

  South Korean President who was gifted jackets by Prime Minister of India which is the very popular trend of today.

Fig. 4.8: South Korean President wearing Modi Jacket

- **Group Size:** Conformity mostly increases with increase in size of the group, but it remains in that direction up to certain limit. In a large group if there is strong agreement among most of the members, then norms also become stronger and the minority more likely to confirm because of stronger group pressure. Thus, if you attend any public function like a speech or a dance, though you don't like it, you give a round of applause because rest of the audience claps. But in this case, as the audience is very big in number, you may choose to go against conformity. But if the performance is in front of just very few people, then in that case conformity is greater.

  According to Rod Bond, 2005, it is argued that normative influence is likely to be stronger when participants make public responses and are face-to-face with the majority, whereas informational influence is likely to be stronger when participants make private responses and communicate with the majority indirectly.
- **Commitment to the group:** Conformity gets affected by the strength with which the individual is committed to the group. The commitment is considered as a force which keeps the person in a relation with group. The more committed the person to a group, greater the conformity. For example, if all the friends from a group decide to dress up based on a theme, then even though few may not like, follow the decision because they are positively committed to the group.
- **Individual Differences:** Whether to follow the trend or not also depends upon personal characteristics. Motivation, values, leadership abilities, openness to experience, etc. are important factors which decide conformity. An individual who strictly follows familial norms may not drink at the party where his other friends are performing that behavior.

4.3.4 Using Conformity for Healthy Behavior

Harnessing the positive effects of conformity could be a great thing for inculcating good habits. With the help of any popular or influential person from sports, entertainment, politics or any other field healthy habits can be enforced. Importance of exercising, avoiding junk food, driving safely, building toilets and using them, giving vaccinations, etc. could be infused.

Fig. 4.9: Use of influential personality for Polio Eradication

When an individual sees large number of people doing it and experiencing positive results, then he also wants to go for conformity.

Social norm marketing is a new approach used by schools which will promote healthy education. (Campo et. al., 2003).

Though, in most of the behavior conformity is seen, there are many people who resist conformity. Factors like individuation (which is a need to be distinguishable from others in some respect), minority influence, etc. force people to resist conformity.

4.3.5 Obedience and Authority

If some officer in uniform asks you to kill someone, would you? You may say, "Obviously not!" But the result of experiments on obedience in social psychology predicts something different. People normally obey the authority. Obedience is extreme yet another form of social influence which occurs as per the direction or order by the other person. In other words, it may be said that, if that direction or order would have not been given, the behavior would have been different.

When the orders or directions to behave in a certain way are given by some authority person, obedience occurs. Hence, it is very obvious that the obedience is dependent on hierarchy and the order is given by the person who hold higher position or status than the one who is receiving order.

The major study on obedience was done by Stanley Milgram in 1960-63. After World War II, when one of the German Military Nazi officials who was responsible for the mass execution of was under trail. Denying responsibly for the mass killing, he said, "I was just following orders from superiors".

Milgram planned an experiment on obedience to find the answer for the question, 'could the Nazi officers' assistance were just to follow orders?' He conducted a series of scientific experiments intended to understand the readiness of a participant to obey the authority. He advertised in the news paper calling people to participate in the experiment and that they would be paid for the same.

Precipitants selected in this way were from various educational backgrounds ranging from school dropouts to doctorates.

The experiment was to be completed in pairs. One used to be is a teacher and the other a student. Both of them were in two separate rooms. The teacher would read a list of words for the student to memorize and if the student makes mistakes, then the teacher would give an electric shock to the student. If the student made more mistakes, the intensity of the electric shock would be increased. The magnitude of the shocks ranged from 15 volts to 450 volts.

Of course, role of student was always played by a confederate, but participants who played teacher were unaware of that. And of course electric shocks were not actually given.

As the experiment progressed, the students used to make mistakes deliberately. Then the teacher who gave shocks used to become upset as they could see students screaming and shouting. Then they used to ask Milgram about what to do next? He used to order those 'teachers' to continue with giving the shocks. The results obtained from this experiment were surprising. Of the total participants, 65% showed complete obedience and gave high intensity shocks. But some refused to continue the experiment.

From this, Milgram concluded that even ordinary person can harm innocent people in observance with the order.

Why do people obey even though they are aware of the consequences of their behavior? Social psychologists have inferred following reasons:

1. People assume that they are just obeying the results and the one who is giving orders is responsible for it.
2. Mostly every one of us have been taught since childhood to follow the orders given by elders and higher officials.
3. People find difficult to disobey or resist the authority which is generally associated with the status symbols like uniform or a badge.
4. People choose to obey as they are afraid of being punished if they disobey.

5. In general, the orders start with lesser extent and gradually the intensity increases.
6. At times of urgency or emergency it happens that there is hardly any time to think and then decide whether to obey or disobey.

4.3.6 Compliance

Have you ever bought dresses or some goods just because the smart salesperson convinced you to do so? Has any shopkeeper told you that he has got attractive deal 'just for you?' Our change in behavior is because of compliance. We mostly comply in many situations because we just want to get out of that situation and it is the most polite way to do so.

In social psychology compliance is defined as follows: "The technique of convincing with a request by an individual is compliance."

Compliance is a very interesting topic of social influence. In social psychology it means changing one's behavior by direction or request of other. In obedience the change of mind or behavior is because of the position of the authority person. But in compliance the behavior change is due to requests by the other person. It is doing what we are asked to do, even though we might not prefer to do.

It is one of the important techniques used in the field of marketing and consumer behavior. Various strategies are used to force the consumer to buy the product. Some of them are as follows:

- **The foot-in-the-door technique:** Under this strategy, the person starts with a small request, which is usually not refused. Once this request is accepted, then the person comes with bigger request. As the other person has accepted small, there are high chances that the bigger request will also get accepted. For example, if your neighbor is going for vacation, then he may ask you to take care of his house in his absence. You accept this small request as you are not doing anything special. Once you accept, he will ask you to water his plants in the garden.

  You may have got a call saying, you have got a surprise gift (mostly free) from some company, once you go and accept the same, the other member of company will ask to invest in something bigger.
- **The door-in-face technique:** In this, the person first begins with a large request, which is assumed to be refused. Once you refuse the bigger, then the smaller, which is the one desired, is made. After refusing bigger request, another person usually accepts the relatively

smaller request. For example, in the above mentioned case, the neighbor will request you to feed his dog when he will be on vacation. But you may refuse it because of the liability and everyday compulsion. If you refuse this request, then he will further request you to at least water his plants in the garden.

- **The deadline technique:** Most of the companies advertise that their product will be available for only very few days, or till the stock is remaining. In fact the company has enough stock of the product remaining, but the psychology of the people is to hurry and purchase the product before they miss. Because, people will buy any product when it is running short, rather than when it is easily available.

4.4 Group Decision Making

The earlier discussion of this chapter talks about social groups like groups of friends, family or like-minded people or colleagues. Though we are members of such groups, hardly we come across with making major decisions which will affect large number of people or any organization, neither they are nationally or internationally important.

In various institutions, organizations, government offices, companies, etc. when there is a problem to be solved or any new strategy is to be implemented, a group is formed which works on that issue and finds solution. Group level decision making has different aspects than individual level.

We make number of decisions everyday such as whether to go to college or stay at home? Whether to drive own vehicle or book a taxi? These are individual level decisions. But when the decisions are made by a formal group, usually they are at organizational or institutional level. For example, the decisions like GST application, or demonetization, etc.

Fig. 4.10: Example of group decision '12 Angry Men'

In 1957, there was an English movie directed by Sidney Lumet named '12 Angry Men'. It was a courtroom drama which told a story of panel of 12 judges who were to decide whether a young defendant is to be punished or not on a reasonable doubt. It is an excellent movie which can be studied from the angle of group decision.

Social psychology is the discipline which is associated with more than two people. Hence when we study the decision making, we must study the process of making a decision by a group which is drastically different by an individual. Study of group decision was initiated by notable psychologists like Kurt Lewin, Mujafer Sherif, and Floyd Allport. Let us study more about group decisions.

4.4.1 Formation of Group

Decisions which are made on individual level affect a very few people, but group level decisions affect larger population. It means, the consequences of decision made individually or as a group member can impact ourselves and to others greatly. Hence it is extremely important to understand and study the process of group formation and decision making.

The formation of group is one of the important steps in decision making. When any group is asked to make a decision, then the way it is constructed plays crucial role. Tuckman has suggested five sequential stages in the process. The ideal way of formation of group is supposed to be as follows:

- **Forming:** It is initial stage which lasts only for few days. Members begin to understand their new roles and plan their work.
- **Storming:** During this stage exchange of ideas, information takes place. As every member feels their idea as unique and superior, there exist considerable arguments and intellectual fights. It is the most critical period of the complete process. Without training, support, and interventions this stage may not be passed successfully. Once this stage is over, the group builds confidence for next stage.
- **Norming:** In this stage, the group builds own norms and begin to trust each other. The members also get skilled in interpersonal relationships, conflicts resolution and problem solving.
- **Performing:** Now the group is ready to perform the respective task and the job assigned, because every member is well acquainted with one another.

- **Adjourning:** This stage comes later, after the task has been completed successfully and the required solution has been found out.

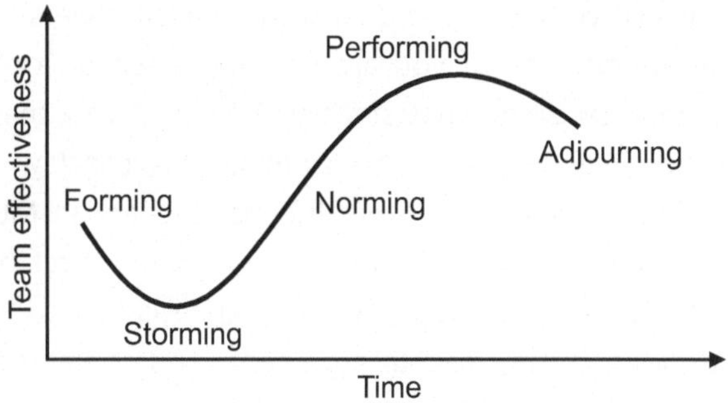

Fig. 4.11: Stages of group formation

4.4.2 Definition of Group Decision Making

Group decision making is the collective activity where many individuals interact, discuss and brainstorm to come to a solution supposedly unanimous. When the process of group decision making starts most of the times, there is no agreement in the opinions of the group members. So it is not necessary that all the group members must agree with each other hence forth.

It is a process or sequence of activities involving stages of problem recognition, search for information, definition of alternatives and selection one from more alternatives. It is an act of evaluating several alternatives and choosing the most suitable one.

- "It is a process which involves combining and integrating available information in order to choose one of the several possible courses of actions." **- Baron and Byrne.**

Group decisions are subject to the factors such as social influence, and group dynamics. In most of the cases it is harder to reach an unanimous decision, but it involves compromises. A group can make decisions by agreement or it may also be made by majority rule.

Groups are seen as superior to individuals as group represents larger and diverse set of experiences and perspectives. Hence group has more potential to be more effective and end up with more creative result.

Though there are basic differences in decision making on individual level and group level, the process takes in three steps common, which are defining the problem, collecting the information and choosing one option out of few.

4.4.3 Stages and Steps in Group Decision Process

Let us understand group decision process with following example. Imagine five of your friends along with yourself have shifted to Mumbai for further studies. All of you are now in search of a place to stay. To come to final decision, what steps you follow? You search for a flat in decent residential area, surf various online sites, check with estate agents, get more information from other friends who are in Mumbai, compare house rents etc. It means on initial stage you collect huge amount of information. In second stage, all of you discuss and brainstorm with various options. It may lead to arguments and sometimes in fights also. After evaluating pros and cones of every option, ultimately all of you get convinced with one option and finalize the same. Likewise, group decisions are made in similar manner on larger scale. But group decision making is not always a smooth process. In order to maximize the potential of this process following steps should be taken:

- **Establish the group goal:** A clear goal statement should be resolved so that the group remains united and cohesion is created. Having concrete and clear goal helps in collaboration.
- **Facilitate a working environment:** Once the clear goal is established, every member of the group must be allowed to work meaningfully and honestly. Open and effective communication facilitates the decision making process.
- **Awareness about expectations and responsibilities:** Every member of the group must be aware of the roles and responsibility attached with it. It helps to ascertain the accountability.
- **Provide resource:** For complete participation of every member of the group in decision making process, they must be provided then required resources.

  To make the process more effective, one important step which could be taken by the in-charge or manager is to stay away from the group, and be present only as strong support. Interference by the superior may harm the team to perform optimally.

Nature of Group Decision

Whether the responsibility of major decisions is to be given to an individual or to a group? Which situation seems to come with less error? Is it true that because in a group more persons are involved, hence the group is supposed to make less errors? Do individuals make safe decisions than riskier?

In 1968, James Stoner argued that groups tend to make relatively dangerous decisions than an individual would make. This is termed as **risky shift**. It occurs when people change their opinions to make more intense decision than when working individually. However, sometimes, group tends to shift towards more cautious decision, which is a conservative shift. To study group decision making process, James Stoner asked participants to make decisions regarding real life happenings first as an individual, then along with group and again to rate as an individual. He noticed that, group decisions were more risky.

When group discussion leads to more extreme decision, the phenomenon is called as **'group polarization'**. There are two major reasons for group polarization. When people hold their belief as an individual, they are not aware of beliefs and opinions of others and assume that they are having better idea. Once they get new information during group discussion, they realize they are too having average idea which is not unique. This **'social comparison'** forces them to move to extreme solution. The social comparison theory was given by Festinger, 1954. According to him it is human nature to want to evaluate our opinions and abilities, and on way to do this is by comparing our views to others.

Another aspect of group decision is **'groupthink'**. It is characterized by a group that feels invulnerable ad is excessively optimist. For example, there was a myth about the very famous ship Titanic that it was unsinkable. Groupthink leads to poor group decision making based on inadequate considerations and alternatives (Taylor, Peplau and Sears, 2006). When all the members of the group are not allowed to express their opinions, the decisions are believed to be unanimous and hence groupthink arises. Also group members don't allow themselves to remain open for the outside information. The group leadership is usually directive in nature.

In addition, groups often get engaged in biased processing of information in order to reach the decisions. It is the tendency of group members to discuss information that is available to all the group members while ignoring equally important information which is available to only few members. This is termed as **shared information bias**.

Considering the nature and threats to group decision following techniques may be followed to reach to healthy group decision.

4.4.5 Techniques of Group Decision

There are several techniques which can be used to get effective group decision. Few of them are as follows-

1. **Brainstorming:** It is a technique where creative ideas and varied views can be gathered through group debate. During this, group members are required to share their ideas or opinions without hesitation.
2. **Nominal group technique:** It is a form of brainstorming, where a planned and well thought-out meeting is conducted with all the group members when they are required to find solution to the identified problem.
3. **Delphi technique**: RAND Cooperation developed this method in 1950s. This technique needs a group of experts who anonymously respond the questionnaires often sent via mails and then they receive feedback. The experts are expected to give justifications for the answers given. The aim is to lessen wide range of responses and arrive at that which could be nearer to expert. This method is advantageous as diverse opinions can be gathered from larger pool of experts. As no data is shared with experts, the responses are true from any influence.
4. **Dialectic decision making:** It is also called Socratic Method. This process helps to better understand all the alternatives with pros and cons. This method ensures generation of alternatives seriously. Though time consuming, this technique brings out greater number of alternative solutions. This method is applicable only in certain situations, but found to be excellent method. It is recommended to use when the situation really demands it.

4.5 Application: Team Building

As we have seen earlier that team is special type of group. The members of this group i.e. the team members have one goal and all of them strive for the same. They not only share commitment to goal, but also a team vision of success. Along with, they provide support to each other which facilitates the mental and physical well being.

It is observed that the lone wolf is becoming an endangered species. As a wolf, if human being also would have been staying alone, probably, we too- a human race would have got extinct. Though exaggerated, but this example indicates the importance of teamwork. The world is extremely complex that no one is competent to stay alone. Realizing this fact long ago, human being started staying in a group. In today's modern world, people need to work collaboratively with different groups of people in their personal as well as professional lives.

When all the members of a group share a common goal, work along with each other, then they are said to form a team.

Fig 4.12 shows the performance of two sports named synchronized swimming and sky diving.

This flawless performance is possible because of strong teamwork.

Fig. 4.12: Examples of team work

4.5.1 Building a Dream Team

Team building is a process of establishing and developing a greater sense of collaboration and trust among the members of a team. If an individual joins any group, then immediately expecting to get well along won't be possible. One needs some time to get adapted with new people, new norms and new working atmosphere. During this developmental period every person faces some sort of difficulties. But once the team has been established, it works efficiently. Therefore, it is important to understand what makes a dream team.

Every person is unique by its nature and temperament. Apparently it may be difficult for most of the people to get well along with other as there are differences in opinions. Thus to build and to maintain a team is a task. According to Suzanne Bell, associate professor, University of Chicago, a team's success often depends upon its composition.

The composition of team may be of two types- surface level and deep level. Surface level characteristics of team members such as age, gender, etc. are of primary importance for overall functioning of the team. But these characters do not matter as significantly as the deep level characteristics matter. Deep level characters like abilities, personality traits, skills, values, etc. are not readily observable. Though these attributes are not seen at a glance, they have great impact on team and its working.

As per Bell, the deep level factors which are ABC of teamwork. These factors are attitude, behavior and cognitive state. These are three basic tenets of team work and its success.

For example, a pessimistic person influences negatively to others. Team members with high morality, are better at self discipline and regulation of team. Members who are willing to adapt, learn, solve problem, etc. are better in working together.

4.5.2 Benefits of Team Building

From corporate or organizational aspect, team development is important not just for the immediate advantage to the company, but also to the team and members for developing group skills, communication and consequent bonding. All organizations can run successfully if they work as a team. To increase efficiency and productivity; formation of strong team is one of the major tasks. To keep all the employee bonded together helps the organization in long run.

In terms of corporate sector, the word team building has become the password to accomplishment. The success of most organizations depends on effective working of strongly bonded employees in the form of team.

Fig. 4.13: Organizations work only if team works

Though the major aim to build a team is to increase productivity and motivation to work together in harmony, there are other significant goals of team building. They are –

- Improves leadership skills.
- Gives awareness regarding expectations and responsibilities of an individual separately and also as a part of team.
- Helps in overcoming the lacunas or shortcoming in an individual when working as team.
- Hidden potential as well as weaknesses of an individual can be identified.
- Organization gets an idea about what factors may be considered as opportunities and what as threats.
- Brings all the members of organization together for common cause, which helps in cultivating sense of belonging.
- Overall running of the organizations occurs harmoniously.

Thus, working as a team has always been proved to be beneficial. Team activities help in making group decisions. As such structured activities not only encourage individuals' development, but also promote growth of an organization.

✧ Exercise ✧

Q. 1 : *Answer the following questions in 100 words :*

(1) *What do you understand by the concept of group dynamics?*

(2) *Define and explain types of groups.*

(3) *What are common bond group and common identity group? Explain with examples.*

(4) *What are the four stages of intergroup experiment in Robber's Cave experiment?*

Q. 2 : *Answer the following questions in 200 words :*

(1) *Elaborate various characteristics of groups.*

(2) *What are the factors affecting cooperation?*

(3) *Discuss the conclusion of Prisoner's dilemma.*

(4) *What is the nature of conflict?*

Q. 3 : *Answer the following questions in 400 words :*

(1) *Discuss the reasons why an individual joins or leaves any group.*

(2) *Explain the importance of Mujafer Sherif's experiment on conformity.*

(3) *What are the strategies of conflict resolution?*

(4) *Why do people obey the authority?*

Q. 4 : *Write short notes :*

(1) *Various techniques in compliance.*

(2) *Tuckman's stages of formation of group.*

(3) *Nature and technique of group decision.*

(4) *Team building.*

✧ Questions from Previous University Exams ✧

(1) *Write a short note on group decision makings.* **(April 2012)**

(2) *Describe factors affecting conformity.* **(April 2012)**

(3) *Write a note on Sherif's experiment on competition and conflict* **(April 2013)**

(4) *What is foot in door technique?* **(October 2013)**

(5) *What is compliance?* **(May 2014)**

(6) *Explain the concept of obedience.* **(April 2016)**

(7) *Explain the group decision making.* **(April 2016)**

☆☆☆

Model Question Paper

F.Y. B.A. : Introduction to Social Psychology

(2019-20 PATTERN)

Hours: 3 **Marks: 70**

Q.1. Answer the following questions in 100 words each: (Any 4) [20]

(i) *What is social cognition?*

(ii) Explain nature of aggression.

(iii) What are the characteristics of a group?

(iv) What is locus of control?

(v) Explain the history of social psychology from Indian context.

(vi) Compare between cooperation and competition.

Q. 2. Answer the following questions in 200 words each: (Any 2) [20]

(i) What are the dimensions of attitudes?

(ii) Explain the prevention and reduction in aggression.

(iii) What are the situational factors in pro-social behavior?

(iv) Explain the triangular theory of love.

Q. 3. Answer the following questions in 400 words: (Any 1) [20]

(i) Describe self-presentation and self-regulation.

(ii) Explain various levels of social behavior.

Q.4. Write short notes: (Any 2) [10]

(i) Prejudice Eradication.

(ii) Internal determinants of interpersonal attraction.

(iii) Benefits of joining a group.

(iv) Team building.

☆☆☆

Reference Books

1. Baron, R. A., Branscombe, N. R., & Byrne, D. Bhardwaj, Gopa. (2008). Social Psychology. (12th Ed.). New Delhi: Pearson Education, Indian subcontinent adaptation 2009.
2. Baron, R. A., Branscombe, N. R., & Byrne, D. Bhardwaj, Gopa. (2008). Social Psychology. (12th ed). New Delhi: Pearson Education, Marathi Translation by Natu Sadhna, Vaidya Alpana, and Rajhans Manasi.
3. Baron, R. A. and Byrne, D. (1997). Social Psychology, 8th edition. Boston, MA: Allyn and Bacon
4. Dalal, A.K. and Mishra, G. (2001). New Directions in Indian Psychology (Vol. 1 : Social Psychology). New Delhi: Sage Publications.
5. Egbert Klautke, The Mind of the Nation: The Debate about Völkerpsychologie, 1851-1900 School of Slavonic and East European Studies, University College London.
6. Gadekar, K.N., Patil, A. & Inamdar, A.K.(2007). Pragat Samajik Manashastra, Pune: Diamond Publication.
7. Blowers G.H.and Turtle, A.M. (eds.), Psychology Moving East: The Status of Western Psychology in Asia and Oceania. Sydney: Sydney University Press, 1987, pp. 362
8. Misra, G. and Dalal A., Psychology for India, 2015, Sage publications, p 260.
9. Sinha, D. Psychology in India: A historical perspective ;
10. Tadsare, Tambake, Patil & Darekar (2003). Samajik Manasshatra, Kolhapur: Phadke Prakashan.
11. https://www.ipi.org.in/texts/ajit/dalal-social-psychology.pdf
12. http://egyankosh.ac.in/bitstream/123456789/20856/1/Unit-4.pdf

☆☆☆